Fundamentals of Statistical Analysis

David Cope
Harvard Law School

Reprinted from
Analytical Methods for Lawyers

© 2005 By FOUNDATION PRESS

　　　　　395 Hudson Street
　　　　　New York, NY 10014
　　　　　Phone Toll Free 1–877–888–1330
　　　　　Fax (212) 367–6799
　　　　　fdpress.com
Printed in the United States of America

ISBN 1–58778–895–0

 TEXT IS PRINTED ON 10% POST
CONSUMER RECYCLED PAPER

For my parents, Julius and Lillian Cope

Preface

This text is intended for smart people who are not especially comfortable with numbers. Its goal is to prepare readers to thoughtfully and critically engage with the sorts of statistically based arguments that are common in real world settings such as law courts, legislatures, government agencies and the press. While full coverage of the field of statistics would require many hundreds of pages covered with complex mathematical symbolism, fortunately, most of the statistical arguments that really matter in practical life are ones that can be usefully explicated in a brief text such as the present one, which utilizes only very elementary mathematics. For those readers with a special interest in the use of statistics in the employment discrimination context, pages 83-96 present a self-contained explanation of the basic statistical methodology relied on in discrimination litigation.

I owe debts to the many Harvard Law Students who used and commented on earlier versions of this material over the past four years; to Sandra Badin for her extremely insightful editorial assistance, to Diane Long for her expert support in the preparation of the manuscript and to Howell Jackson, Steve Shavell, Louis Kaplow and Kip Viscusi for their intellectual camaraderie which made developing the Analytical Methods course, for which this text was originally prepared, such a pleasure.

Cambridge, MA
January 2005

Contents

I

Statistical Analysis

Statistics is the science of collecting, organizing, and interpreting numerical facts — that is, data.[1] Though the science of statistics is a broad and deep area of study that can be the subject of multiple year long classes, the core of statistics consists of a relatively small subset of arguments and techniques which allow for the performance of three fundamental tasks: effectively organizing and describing sets of data, using current data to make predictions about future events or patterns of events, and using data to help confirm or disconfirm hypotheses about the way the world works.

As we shall see, statistical claims, though typically presented in courts as resulting from the strict application of scientific methodology, often depend on the exercise of a good deal of subjective judgement on the part of the particular statistician or analyst making them. Knowledge of where such subjectivity enters is crucial to the effective critique of such claims. A major goal of this handbook is to make plain for you the logic supporting the various forms of statistical argumentation and so enable you to recognize where methodology leaves off and subjectivity begins.

---

1. The word *statistics* actually has three separate but related meanings. When used as the name of a discipline, as in *if you study statistics, you'll be a more effective lawyer*, it has the meaning given in the text. A second, often encountered, meaning is a reference to numbers that can be analyzed using the science of statistics, as in *each year, the Justice Department publishes statistics on the incidence of all types of felonies*. A third technical meaning of statistics will be introduced later in the chapter.

1. One-Variable Descriptive Statistics

How have mutual funds performed over the past year? This question can be answered in a number of ways. For example, a list of all mutual funds and their yields for the year could be compiled. In fact, major newspapers (e.g., the *New York Times* and the *Wall Street Journal*) do just this, and the list takes up five or more pages, even though it's printed in very small type. Despite the huge amount of information that the list contains, for many purposes

---

Box 1
Scientific Experts

A recent development in the law of evidence has made statistics more important than ever before to litigators. In *Daubert v. Merrell Dow*, 509 U.S. 579 (1993), the Court held that judges were to act as gatekeepers for scientific evidence: judges would review the scientific methods underlying proffered evidence, and only if they deemed the methods acceptable could the evidence be introduced at trial. Often, at least one of the critical methodological issues to be reviewed is a matter of statistics. Later cases — *General Electric Co. v. Joiner*, 522 U.S. 136 (1996), and *Kumho Tire Co. v. Carmichael*, 526 U.S. 137 (1999) — have expanded the scope of the *Daubert* review to cover all expert testimony. *Daubert* and its progeny represent the Supreme Court's attempt to come to grips with the problem of so-called "junk science" in the courtroom — wherein impressionable juries decide cases on the basis of nonstandard "science" presented by hired experts with impressive credentials. The problem is still common, however, in large part because most judges are untutored in the scientific methods that they've been delegated to police.

---

it isn't very helpful. Suppose that you're thinking about investing in a particular fund and want to compare its performance last year with that of mutual funds overall before making your decision. The complete list wouldn't be of much help unless you spent a lot of time organizing and summarizing the information in it. The newspapers spare their readers this onerous task by providing a variety of summaries, in words, numbers, and pictures. (Remarkably, one of these summaries encapsulates the entire body of information in a single number: the average rate of return for all mutual funds for the year.) Most readers use the list itself only to look up the performance of a few funds that they're particularly interested in. Then they turn their attention to the summaries, which they're likely to find much more useful.

Many other questions that arise every day invite similar treatment: What was the starting salary for last year's law school graduates? How much do female engineers earn? What is the prognosis for Hodgkin's disease patients treated with chemotherapy? Although a list of the available information would be of some value in each case, one or more summaries would probably better serve the questioner. Even where data sets are small, the old saying "a picture is worth a thousand words" (or in this case, a thousand *numbers*) will often be true. Data presented in a well chosen graphic or pictorial form will typically be much more easily assimilable (and rhetorically persuasive if that is your purpose) than the same data presented in simple tabular form. Hence the ubiquity in newspapers, journals, books, and classrooms of a wide variety of statistical graphics.

A. Making Sense of Data

No concept is more basic to descriptive statistics (indeed, to all of statistics) than that of *data*. For the purposes of statistics, data are just bits of information presented in terms of *individuals* and *variables*. Individuals are the things that the information is *about*. Any object of study can be an individual: a person, a school, a state (e.g., Alabama), an act (e.g., arson), and so forth. A variable can be any *property* of individuals under study, as long as the individuals differ in some way with respect to the property and their differences can in some practical way be measured or ascertained. Height can be a variable because rulers, yardsticks, etc. offer practical ways of measuring it. Greediness, though a property of individuals, cannot function as a variable unless an investigator devises a practical way of measuring it. An investigator who develops such a measurement technique is said to have *operationalized* the concept of greediness. (If a law professor wants

Table 1
Quantitative Variable: Five-Year Rates of Return for a Group of Mutual Funds (hypothetical data)

Load mutual fund	5-Year rate of return (%)	No-load mutual fund	5-Year rate of return (%)
AIM Advisor	16.20	Accessor	21.90
American Express	26.70	American Century	9.50
BB&T Growth	21.10	Excelsior	24.30
Chase Vista	21.70	Fidelity Puritan	15.10
DU Winthrop	10.00	Heartland Value	12.50
Dreyfus Premier	-8.00	Janus Enterprise	23.80
Fidelity Select	18.30	J.P. Morgan US	13.00
Galaxy Equity	18.40	Meridian Fund	12.70
Guardian	23.60	Mutual Beacon	17.40
Kemper	9.00	PIMCO Stocks Plus	16.40
Lexington Strategic	-11.00	Ryders OTC	40.90
MainStay	22.40	Standish Equity	19.30
MFS Research	21.20	T. Rowe Price Equity	20.70
One Group	21.90	Vanguard Utilities	-16.60
Parkstone	9.70	Westcore	15.80
Principal Balanced	12.80		
Smith Barney	21.30		
United Continental	12.30		
Van Eck Gold	-14.20		
Zwieg Strategy	10.50		

Table 2
Categorical Variable:
Homicides by Chosen Weapon, 1998

Type of weapon	No. of homicides
Handgun	7,361
Knife	1,877
Fist	949
Blunt object	741
Shotgun	619
Rifle	538

Source: *Uniform Crime Reports* (1999).

to use statistical methods to test the hypothesis that the sociability of law students is correlated with their job choices, she would first have to operationalize sociability. Can you think of a way she might do this?)

Variables come in two types. A variable that's measured numerically, such as height, weight, blood pressure, GPA, or price, is a *quantitative variable*. In Table 1, for example, five-year rate of return is a quantitative variable. A variable that requires that each individual be assigned to one of several specified or implied categories, such as gender, race, or marital status, on the other hand, is a *categorical variable*. In Table 2, chosen weapon is a categorical variable.

A collection of values of a given variable for more than one individual is a *one-variable data set*. Table 1 presents a one-variable data set, Table 2 presents a summary of another one-variable data set. (What does the one-variable data set summarized in Table 2 look like?) Combining two or more one-variable data sets for the same individuals produces a *multivariate data set* (see Table 3). The number of variables in a multivariate data set can be very large. The U.S. Census, for example, consists of hundreds of data points for each individual surveyed. Picturing, analyzing, and applying data become increasingly difficult as the number of vari-

Table 3
A Multivariate Data Set: Education, Income, and Poverty

| County | Public school enrollment Fall | | | Educational attainment, 1990 Percent | | |
	1998-1999	1994-1995	1990	Persons 25 years and over	High school graduate or higher	Bachelor's degree or higher
Maine	210,080	212,225	212,465	795,613	78.8	18.8
Androscoggin	16,472	17,438	17,664	66,785	71.8	12.6
Aroostook	13,349	14,653	16,509	55,738	70.9	12.5
Cumberland	39,693	37,475	37,559	159,876	85.0	27.6
Franklin	5,348	5,471	5,575	17,980	79.7	17.7
Hancock	8,198	8,354	7,565	31,475	83.3	21.4
Kennebec	18,361	18,735	20,441	74,858	78.9	18.1
Knox	4,744	4,842	5,837	24,778	80.8	19.8
Lincoln	6,236	6,353	5,037	20,674	81.4	22.2
Oxford	10,673	10,585	9,814	34,779	76.9	12.7
Penobscot	24,571	25,473	24,756	91,410	79.1	17.7
Piscataquis	3,173	3,473	4,057	12,248	75.4	12.3
Sagadahoc	6,952	6,991	5,885	21,573	81.1	21.6
Somerset	9,316	9,821	10,066	31,726	71.9	10.5
Waldo	5,240	5,226	6,404	21,295	77.4	16.8
Washington	5,428	6,359	6,777	23,087	73.2	12.7
York	32,326	31,276	28,519	107,331	79.5	19.0
Maryland	841,671	790,938	703,379	3,122,665	78.4	26.5
Allegany	10,978	11,303	10,872	49,857	71.0	11.8
Anne Arundel	74,079	70,588	63,918	276,130	81.1	24.6
Baltimore	105,914	99,231	85,386	473,574	78.4	25.0
Calvert	15,241	12,819	9,659	32,408	79.3	17.6
Caroline	5,685	5,290	4,616	17,510	66.8	10.8
Carroll	27,224	24,515	21,115	79,153	78.5	19.6
Cecil	15,550	14,258	12,628	44,944	72.2	12.1
Charles	22,263	20,419	18,228	60,821	81.0	16.2
Dorchester	5,143	5,165	4,821	20,861	64.7	10.9
Frederick	35,383	31,655	26,088	94,994	80.4	22.0
Garrett	5,082	5,104	5,306	17,908	68.4	9.5
Harford	38,909	35,956	30,153	115,199	81.6	21.5
Howard	41,858	36,125	29,545	122,454	91.1	46.9
Kent	2,891	2,794	2,595	11,822	81.4	16.9
Montgomery	127,933	117,082	101,083	512,839	90.6	49.9
Prince George's	130,259	118,478	106,064	458,296	83.2	25.5
Queen Anne's	6,888	6,020	5,498	22,993	76.8	19.9
St. Mary's	14,743	13,428	12,800	45,592	77.1	16.8
Somerset	3,113	3,339	3,698	15,901	61.2	9.6
Talbot	4,590	4,340	3,829	21,903	76.5	23.0
Washington	20,159	19,510	18,459	81,140	69.3	11.4
Wicomico	14,330	13,652	11,738	47,231	72.1	18.5
Worcester	6,916	6,439	5,241	24,828	70.8	14.8
Independent city						
Baltimore city	106,540	113,428	110,039	474,307	60.7	15.5
Massachusetts	937,647	893,727	830,138	3,965,223	80.0	27.2
Barnstable	28,788	30,964	26,042	133,951	88.4	28.1
Berkshire	15,802	21,204	20,346	92,609	77.9	20.9
Bristol	84,296	82,475	80,028	327,994	65.0	15.9
Dukes	2,543	2,182	1,796	8,245	90.4	32.1
Essex	116,844	105,625	94,592	445,994	80.2	25.9
Franklin	11,907	11,813	10,925	46,559	82.4	24.2
Hampden	77,037	71,919	69,898	292,806	73.6	17.6
Hampshire	20,100	20,772	18,531	85,463	83.0	31.9
Middlesex	206,094	189,963	177,247	941,201	84.3	35.4
Nantucket	1,238	1,042	764	4,316	89.4	32.9
Norfolk	95758	88154	77929	421102	88.0	34.4
Plymouth	78989	77360	73465	276957	83.8	22.2
Suffolk	79,258	73,551	72,355	427,138	85.4	27.7
Worcester	118,993	116,703	106,220	457,888	77.4	22.2

Median household income			Persons below poverty level, 1997				
			Number			Percent	
		Percent	Persons of all ages		Persons	Person	Persons
1997	1989	change,		Net change,	under	of all	under
(dollars)	(dollars)	1989-1997	Total	1989-1997	18 years	ages	18 years
33,140	27,854	19.0	132,809	4,343	44,122	0.7	14.9
34,242	26,979	26.9	10,732	−840	3,575	10.7	14.5
29,124	22,230	31.0	11,152	−724	3,562	15.0	19.6
41,393	32,286	28.2	20,432	1,660	6,366	8.1	11.3
30,712	24,432	25.7	3,643	163	1,247	12.7	17.6
33,397	25,247	32.3	4,974	428	1,626	10.1	14.5
35,559	28,616	24.3	12,040	576	4,046	10.6	14.7
33,478	25,405	31.8	4,050	−149	1,347	10.8	15.5
35,696	28,373	25.8	3,067	184	1,117	9.6	15.3
30,688	24,535	25.1	6,663	219	2,313	12.3	17.4
33,574	26,631	26.1	17,229	−866	5,486	12.1	16.4
28,599	22,132	29.2	2,488	−312	850	13.6	19.1
39,991	31,948	25.2	2,795	410	980	7.8	11.0
28,300	22,829	24.0	7,840	768	2,806	14.9	20.6
29,812	23,148	28.8	5,279	80	1,820	14.3	19.5
25,673	19,993	28.4	6,252	−348	2,106	17.7	24.5
39,288	32,432	21.1	14,173	3,094	4,875	8.0	11.3
45,289	39,386	15.0	484,987	99,691	194,703	9.5	14.9
28,794	21,546	33.6	11,209	−656	4,011	15.9	24.2
56,147	45,147	24.4	24,894	6,503	11,893	5.3	9.7
44,715	38,837	15.1	54,891	17,737	20,936	7.6	12.8
57,017	47,608	19.8	4,815	2,161	2,212	6.6	10.4
32,902	27,758	18.5	3,772	652	1,649	12.8	20.4
55,906	42,378	31.9	7,320	2,792	2,996	4.9	7.2
44,650	36,019	24.0	7,375	2,169	3,359	9.0	14.2
54,110	46,415	16.6	8,757	3,750	4,407	7.4	12.2
29,361	24,922	17.8	4,629	414	1,825	15.5	25.3
53,415	41,382	29.1	10,695	3,640	4,448	5.8	8.6
30,197	22,733	32.8	4,605	563	1,957	15.8	24.2
52,231	41,680	25.3	13,841	4,719	5,813	6.4	9.6
68,024	54,348	25.2	10,503	4,719	4,187	4.4	6.6
36,391	30,104	20.9	1,949	6	703	10.7	17.1
62,130	54,089	14.9	47,141	15,490	18,201	5.6	8.8
47,882	43,127	11.0	71,557	30,275	30,164	9.3	15.1
48,226	39,190	23.1	3,016	781	1,151	7.5	11.3
49,495	37,158	33.2	7,628	2,235	3,528	8.8	13.2
26,867	23,379	14.9	4,344	1,179	1,453	21.8	29.1
39,663	31,885	24.4	3,224	660	1,208	9.7	16.7
37,327	29,632	26.0	12,284	1,710	4,762	10.1	15.7
34,827	28,512	22.1	10,793	2,214	4,431	13.5	21.6
32,815	27,586	19.0	5,106	1,323	2,119	11.9	21.8
27,713	24,045	15.3	150,937	−5,347	57,290	23.7	34.4
43,015	36,952	16.4	649,293	129,954	250,244	10.7	17.0
40,791	31,766	28.4	18,547	4,751	6,912	8.9	15.5
37,284	30,470	22.4	14,783	3,223	5,577	11.3	18.2
38,866	31,520	23.3	61,556	16,389	25,043	11.9	18.8
50,852	31,994	27.7	931	162	319	6.7	10.1
44,187	37,913	16.5	74,648	13,877	29,994	10.6	17.0
38,330	30,350	26.3	7,461	838	2,922	10.5	16.5
36,746	31,100	18.2	72,537	15,200	31,647	16.6	26.9
42,287	34,154	23.8	12,798	−886	3,500	9.4	11.3
53,268	43,847	21.5	103,324	20,385	33,979	7.3	10.9
48,151	40,331	19.4	340	—	106	4.2	6.0
54,528	46,215	18.0	32,148	5,013	9,828	5.0	7.0
49,165	40,905	20.2	40,461	12,308	16,935	8.6	13.2
36,260	29,399	23.3	129,133	14,385	51,621	20.7	35.4
40,489	35,774	13.2	80,628	24,011	31,862	11.1	16.8

ables in a data set increases, though spreadsheets and statistics programs are now available to perform the necessary calculations.

B. Histograms and Frequency Distributions

A one-variable quantitative data set can be represented pictorially in several ways. The type of picture most commonly used by statisticians is a kind of bar graph called a *histogram*. Histograms are such useful tools for describing and analyzing data that statisticians, as an early step in analyzing a data set, routinely construct and scrutinize a histogram for each quantitative variable contained in it.

Let's see how histograms are constructed:

How to . . .

  . . . construct a histogram (using the data in Table-1)

  1. We define and list the names of sufficient equal-sized categories to allow every score in the data set to be placed into one and only one category.[2] Let's use seven categories, those listed in Table 4.

  2. Next, we tally the number of scores that fall into each category and note the tallies next to their respective category names to create a table called a *frequency distribution*.[3] (As used here, frequency means the number of values in a given category.)

  3. We label the horizontal axis (x-axis) of a graph with the name of the variable and its unit of measurement (which in our example are five-year rate of return and percent, respec-

---

2. There is no "right" number of categories to use in creating a histogram, but a good starting point is the square root of the number of individuals in the data set.

3. A variation in histogram construction of which you should be aware is the use of a probability distribution table giving the percentage of individuals in the data set who fall into each category, instead of the actual number of the individuals in each category as in the frequency distribution table. The resulting histograms look the same whether a probability distribution table or a frequency distribution table is used in their construction.

Table 4
Five-Year Rates of Return for a Group of
Mutual Funds: Frequency Distribution

| Five-year rate of return | | No. of |
At least	But less than	funds
−20%	−10%	3
−10%	0%	1
0%	10%	3
10%	20%	15
20%	30%	12
30%	40%	0
40%	50%	1

tively) and mark off a scale that appropriately reflects the category boundaries. We label the the vertical axis (y-axis) frequency, note the unit of measurement (i.e., number of mutual funds), and mark off a scale appropriate for the frequencies (number of scores) in the various categories of our distribution.

4. Our last step is to construct, for each category, a column that spans its interval along the x-axis and extends upward from the x-axis to the level on the y-axis that reflects the frequency for the category. The bars will be proportional in height and area to the frequencies for the categories they represent. (See Figure 1.)

Figure 1
Five-Year Rates of Return for Selected
Publicly Traded Mutual Funds: Histograms

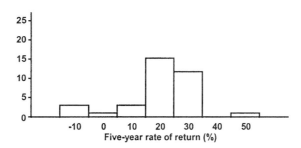

Figure 2
A Rectangular Histogram

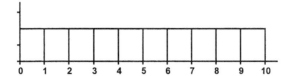

What does a statistician look for when inspecting a histogram? The answer is, first and foremost, its shape — more specifically, an approximate match between the histogram's overall shape and the shape of one of the entries in the statistician's mental catalog of ideal shapes that histograms often resemble.

One simple ideal shape is the rectangle. The histogram in Figure 2 is an example of a rectangular histogram, the graphic equivalent of a *rectangular distribution*. (What can you say about a data set whose histogram resembles a rectangle?)

A more interesting shape in the statisticians' mental catalog is the one in Figure 3: the *normal curve*, which is the graphic equivalent of a *normal distribution*. We can't expect a histogram of an actual data set to look exactly like a normal curve. After all, a normal curve is smooth because it's an ideal shape, whereas a histogram, any histogram, is bumpy, because, by definition, it's made up of columns. So, the most we can expect is for the

Figure 3
A Normal Curve

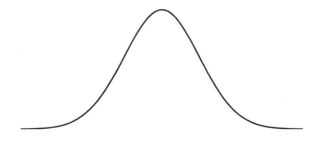

histogram's overall shape to more or less resemble a normal curve (see Figure 4). The degree to which a histogram resembles a normal curve is of great interest: if the distribution of the data portrayed in the histogram matches a normal distribution well enough to be accepted and treated as such, a number of important practical consequences follow. We'll go into these later in the chapter.

Figure 4
A Histogram Resembling a Normal Curve

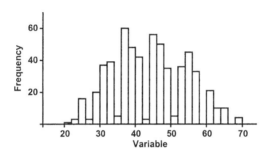

Even when the shape of a histogram doesn't come anywhere near matching an ideal shape, it's amenable to description in statistical language. For example, in contrast to a normal curve (which can be divided into two mirror-image halves by an appropriately placed line and thus is symmetric), some histograms are highly asymmetric. Such a histogram may be either right-skewed or left-skewed (see Figure 5). A histogram constructed from data on income, for example, is likely to be right-skewed. (Why?) One constructed from scores on an easy multiple-choice test, on the other hand, is almost certain to be left-skewed. (Why?)

Another feature of overall histogram shape that statisticians pay attention to is "hilliness." Some histograms are relatively flat, while mounds, or peaks, are obvious in some others. These mounded histograms can be further characterized on the basis of the number of mounds that are apparent: a one-mound histogram is *unimodal*, a two-mound histogram is *bimodal* (see Figure 6), and

Box 2
The Impact of Alternative Forms of Presentation

The way in which data are presented can have a profound effect on the impact that they will have. Any given data set can be presented in myriad ways, and the presentations can vary drastically from one another in appearance. Because all are representations of the same data, it might be tempting to think that differences in appearance are merely cosmetic. But appearance can — and often does — make a crucial difference. Consider the table and the two bar graphs below — three different presentations of the same data. Bar Graph B is a standard unbiased pictorial representation of the data in table A. Bar Graph C presents the same data using a common graphic trick (the y-axis scale does not go to zero). It's a fair bet that graph C would convey a more positive impression of revenue growth than either the table or graph B to most audiences. The enormous persuasive effect that cleverly crafted images of data can have on unsuspecting consumers, such as jurors and voters, has been recognized for the past hundred years or so. In response, a whole field of pictorial representation and misrepresentation has developed. It behooves lawyers presenting quantitative information to be as sensitive to the rhetorical nuances of visual representations of data as they are to those of verbal descriptions of the same basic set of facts. (If you'd like to explore this topic further, the books by Hamilton, Jones, and Tufte cited at the end of the chapter would be good starting points.)

A.

Year	Revenues
1998	$50,000,000
1999	$50,500,000
2000	$51,500,000
2001	$52,500,000
2002	$53,500,000

B.

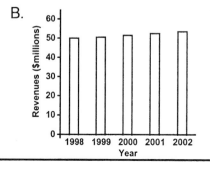

C.

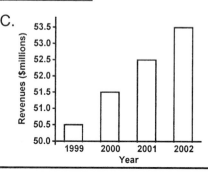

Figure 5
Skewed Histograms

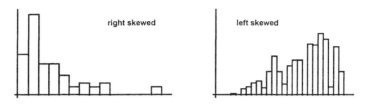

so on.[4] A histogram reflecting the heights of students in a law school classroom is likely to be bimodal. (Why?) What about a histogram that represents years of post-operative survival for 50-year-old male patients who have undergone risky, but potentially lifesaving heart surgery? Multimodality is often a clue that the data have been gathered from subpopulations that differ from one another in some important way.

In addition to looking at the overall shape of a histogram, a statistician checks for *gaps* and *outliers*. A gap naturally raises the question of why few scores (or none at all) have values in that

Figure 6
A Bimodal Histogram

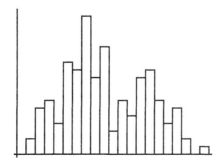

_____

4. *"Modal"* is used in this context because the most frequently occurring score in a distribution is called the *mode* of the distribution.

particular range. Outliers are values much lower or higher than the other values in a data set. Sometimes they're the result of measurement error (due to the use of a broken measuring instrument, for example, or to the misreading of a question by a survey participant), in which case statisticians may decide to exclude the outliers from the analysis. But sometimes outliers are legitimate, "real" scores. They're simply a reflection of the fact that, for the variable in question, extreme values, though rare, do occur. Outliers are a concern because of the very large effects that they can have on the results of formal statistical calculations. Whether to retain or to discard outliers from a particular analysis is a decision that has to be made case by case.

C. Numerical Descriptors/Summaries of Distributions

Two sorts of numerical descriptors of distributions are in common use: measures of central tendency and measures of variability.

1. Measures of central tendency. Very often, a description of a distribution includes a measure of its central tendency (i.e., its center, or average), most commonly its *mean* or *median*. The mean is just the arithmetic average of the values in the distribution. More formally, the mean of a distribution consisting of n values $x_1, x_2, \ldots, x_n$ is

$$(x_1 + x_2 + \ldots + x_n)/n$$

The *median* on the other hand is just the middle value in a distribution, or, if the distribution contains an even number of values, the average of the middle two values.

The mean and median are both in common use. Does it matter which one is reported as a measure of central tendency? For a perfectly symmetric distribution, the answer is no, for the simple reason that the mean and the median are the same: both are equal to the value at the exact center of the distribution. Such is not the case for a skewed distribution, however. As can be seen in Fig-

Figure 7
Mean and Median in a Skewed Distribution

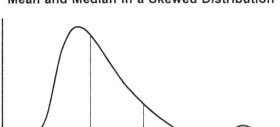

ure 7, in a skewed distribution the mean shifts away from the location of most of the values to a value in the direction of the skew, whereas the median remains near the range of values where the majority of data points are concentrated. This disparity reflects a fundamental difference between the mean and the median — means are much more responsive than are medians to the presence of unusually high or low scores in a distribution. So, if a measure that represents the majority of the data and isn't influenced by a few unusual scores is suitable to the purpose at hand, the median is a better choice than the mean. Indeed, it's the median that's typically reported for well-known skewed distributions, such as housing prices and salaries. Otherwise, the mean is usually more appropriate, because it's sensitive to all scores in the distribution and also, as we'll soon see, because it plays so central a role in inferential statistics. (What's your best guess at the shape of the distribution of wrongful death tort damages? Would the mean of this distribution be a useful summary statistic?)

An example will help to illustrate the importance of the difference between the mean and the median.

Example 1

Mary Starchway, the president of Starchway Cookies, is defending against a claim of gender discrimination in pay at her company. The company has 20 employees (including Ms. Starchway), 10 men and 10 women. Ms. Starchway reports that the average (mean) salary is the same for the men and the women at her company: $60,000. In reviewing the salaries, listed in Table 5, you note that the median is $40,000 for the women but $50,000 for the men. Do either the means or the medians reasonably represent these salary data? When Ms. Starchway gives herself, but no one else, a raise next year, what will happen to these averages? Does it look as if there might be gender discrimination in wages at Starchway Cookies?

Table 5
Example 8-1: Current Salaries of Starchway Employees

Gender	Salary ($000s)									
Men	25	25	50	50	50	50	75	75	100	100
Women	20	20	20	40	40	40	50	50	70	250

An important moral to derive from Example 1 is that when you're presented with an argument that relies on quantitative data it can be a very bad idea for you to be satisfied with a summary statistic such as the mean or the median (or even both), for it will often fail to reveal critical features of the data. Rather, and especially in adversarial situations, you should insist on inspecting the actual data (perhaps in the form of a histogram or dot plot) from which the summary statistics have been derived.

2. Measures of variability or spread. The values in some distributions are bunched very tightly around a central value, while those in others are widely dispersed (see Figure 8). When values are tightly bunched within a narrow range, either the mean or the median may provide a reasonable description of the data. As variability increases (i.e., as the scores spread out over an increasingly large range), the mean and the median become less useful

Figure 8
Data Dispersion

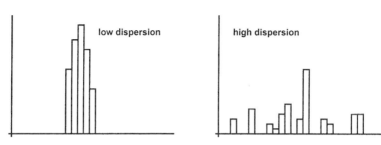

as summaries, because, on average, they fall further and further away from the individual scores. For this reason, statisticians and researchers commonly supplement a measure of central tendency with a measure of the dispersion of the data.

One measure of dispersion, the simplest one, is the *range*, which is simply the difference between the lowest and the highest values in the data set. (What's the range for the Starchway salaries?) However, as a descriptor, the range is severely limited, because it provides little or no information about the majority of the data points. Data sets can have the same range even though their distributions bear very little resemblance to one another.

The most frequently used measure of variability, the *standard deviation*, reflects all of the values in a data set and thus is more sensitive than the range. Let's work through an example to get a better feel for how the standard deviation is calculated and to see one way in which it can be used.

Example 2

Hector is thinking about investing in some of the large-cap common stocks on the Ames Stock Exchange, but he's concerned about the potential risks of such an investment. He wants to know how much variability there was in the returns on these stocks last year. The standard deviation is what he needs, and we will calculate it for him from the data in Table 6. (You'll probably want to follow along in Table 7 as we do the calculations.)

Table 6
Example 2: Last Year's Returns on All Large-Cap
Common Stocks on the Ames Stock Exchange

Stock	Investment return (%)	Stock	Investment return (%)
1	+16	6	+28
2	−1	7	−5
3	+12	8	+12
4	+11	9	+9
5	+8	10	+10

1. To begin, we calculate last year's mean return for all Ames large-cap common stocks, and we find that it's 10%.

2. For each stock, we subtract the mean return, 10%, from its actual return to get its deviation (see Figure 9).

3. We square each stock's deviation.

4. We add all the squared deviations and find that the total is 720.

5. We divide the sum of the squared deviations, 720, by the number of stocks, 10. The result is 72, which is the average (mean) of the squared deviations or *variance*. (What would the result have been if we had averaged the deviations themselves rather than the squared deviations?)

6. Our last step is to find the square root of the variance, 72. This yields the standard deviation, which turns out to be about 8.5.

Figure 9
Example 2: Deviation from the Mean

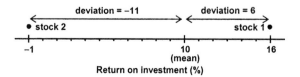

Table 7
Example 2: Calculating the Standard Deviation for Last Year's Returns on All Large-Cap Common Stocks on the Ames Stock Exchange

Stoc	Score value	Score value − = Deviation	Squared deviation
1	+16	+16 − 10 = 6	6^2 = 36
2	−1	−1 − 10 = −11	-11^2 = 121
3	+12	+12 − 10 = 2	2^2 = 4
4	+11	+11 − 10 = 1	1^2 = 1
5	+8	+8 − 10 = −2	-2^2 = 4
6	+28	+28 − 10 = 18	18^2 = 324
7	−5	−5 − 10 = −15	-15^2 = 225
8	+12	+12 − 10 = 2	2^2 = 4
9	+9	+9 − 10 = −1	-1^2 = 1
10	+10	+10 − 10 = 0	0^2 = 0

$\underline{100}$ (sum of score values) $\underline{720}$ (sum of squared deviations)

100 / 10 = 10 (mean)   720 / 10 = 72 (mean squared deviation)

$\sqrt{72} \approx 8.5$ (standard deviation)

These days, fortunately, such calculations are generally done by computers. Doing them manually a couple of times is useful, though, because we're able to see just which characteristic features of a distribution are actually reflected in its standard deviation. Notice in the example that we just worked through, for instance, that almost all of the variability reflected in the standard deviation derives from three data points, those for stocks 2, 6, and 7. That these three data points are outliers is very obvious when we look at Figure 10, a dot plot of Hector's data.

It should be clear from this example that the standard deviation, like the mean, is very responsive to the presence of unusually high or low values in a distribution. Example 3 is a problem for you to tackle on your own.

Figure 10
Outliers in Example 2

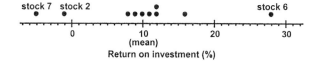

Return on investment (%)

Example 3

Last year's returns on small-cap stocks from the Ames Stock Exchange are listed in Table 8. What's the standard deviation? (Do the calculation by hand.) Make a dot plot of the data. Are there outliers? If the small-cap stocks and the large-cap stocks on the Ames Stock Exchange continue to perform as they did last year, according to the data used in our two examples, what are the relative merits of investing in Ames small-cap and large-cap stocks?

Summing up . . .

To compute a standard deviation

1. For a data set of n scores with values $x_1, x_2, \ldots x_n$, subtract the mean of the scores from the value of each score to find the score's deviation from the mean. (For simplicity, *deviation from the mean* will from now on be shortened to *deviation*.)

Table 8
Example 3: Last Year's Returns on All Small-Cap
Common Stocks on the Ames Stock Exchange

Stock	Investment return (%)	Stock	Investment return (%)
1	+14	6	+14
2	+28	7	−24
3	+16	8	+17
4	+11	9	+30
5	−13	10	+17

2. Square each deviation.

3. Add all the squared deviations.

4. Divide the sum of the squared deviations by n to get the average squared deviation, or variance, of the data set.

5. Find the square root of the variance. The result is the standard deviation.

Generalizations about the standard deviation

1. The standard deviation measures spread about the mean and thus should be used only in conjunction with a reported mean.

2. Like the mean, the standard deviation isn't a "resistant" measure; it's heavily influenced by outliers.

3. The standard deviation equals zero only when all the scores in the data set have the same value.

4. Chebychev's Rule: for any data set, at least 75% of the data points lie within 2 standard deviations of the mean (i.e., within the range bounded by the mean minus 2 standard deviations and the mean plus 2 standard deviations) and at least 89% lie within 3 standard deviations of the mean.[5] (Does this rule hold for the Ames Stock Exchange data?)

---

5. This rule is named after Pafnuty Chebychev, a nineteenth-century Russian mathematician.

D. The Normal Distribution

Researchers are often interested in determining where a given data point falls relative to the others in a data set. They could get at least a rough idea from Chebychev's Rule, but predictions based on the shape of a distribution are likely to be more accurate. When a distribution's shape resembles the ideal normal curve closely enough for the distribution to be treated as normal — and in practice, distributions are very commonly assumed to be approximately normal — predictions about where particular values fall relative to others can be quite accurate.

The normal distribution, rather than being a single distribution, is actually a family of distributions, which look quite similar when represented graphically as curves. The reason for the resemblance is that the curves are derived from very similar mathematical formulas that differ only in the values of 2 variables, the mean and the standard deviation. For each possible combination of mean and standard deviation, there's a unique normal distribution, which, when graphed, produces a version of the familiar bell-shaped curve. A common practice is to use the notation $N(\mu,\sigma)$, where μ ('mu') is the mean and σ ('sigma') is the standard deviation, to designate individual normal distributions. For example, $N(7,5)$ would be a reference to the normal distribution with mean 7 and standard deviation 5. The larger the standard deviation of any given normal distribution relative to its mean, the more spread out the distribution looks when it's represented graphically as a curve (see Figure 11).

While true normal distributions are theoretical constructs representing unrealistic ideals, they and their graphic counterparts, normal curves, are central in statistics, because, as it turns out, many naturally occurring distributions resemble (i.e., approximate) true normal distributions and are treated as if they are, and because, as we shall see, they play an important role in the

Figure 11
Two Members of the Family of Normal Curves

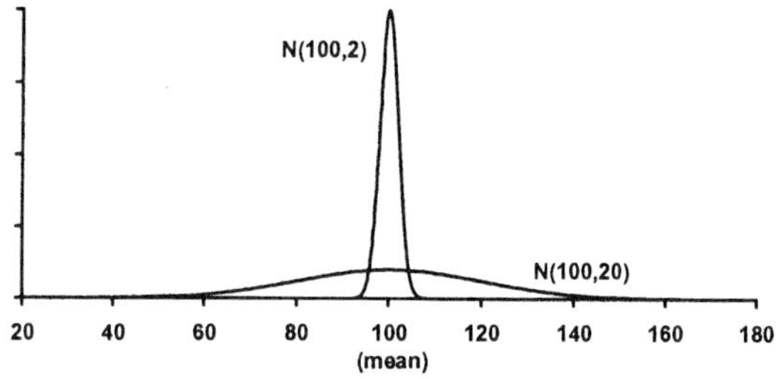

theory of hypothesis testing and estimation.. The decision that a distribution is "normal enough" is a powerful assumption. All inferences based on it are only as valid as the assumption itself.[6]

Properties of . . .

. . . normal distributions and normal curves

1. All normal curves are similar in appearance, bell shaped and symmetric.

2. The mean, the median, and the mode of every normal distribution have the same value: mean = median = mode. (The mode is the most frequently occurring value in the distribution and corresponds to the highest point of the curve.)

3. The 68%–95%–99.7% Rule: in every normal distribution, about 68% of the values are within 1 standard deviation of the mean (i.e., within the range bounded by the mean minus 1 standard deviation and the mean plus 1 standard

---

6. A natural question is: How close to being perfectly normally distributed must the data be for them to be considered normally distributed? This issue is often a crucial one for statisticians, and complex tests have been devised to assess the precise degree of the match, or *fit*, between the distribution of any given data and the normal distribution. Nevertheless, even though such a determination can be made, deciding whether to accept any particular degree of fit as "close enough" is a matter of judgment, not method, with due consideration given to the purpose of the analysis at hand.

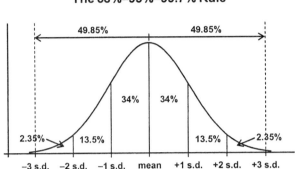

Figure 12
The 68%–95%–99.7% Rule

deviation), about 95% are within 2 standard deviations, and about 99.7% are within 3 standard deviations (see Figure 12).[7]

The 68%–95%–99.7% Rule enables us to solve an interesting class of problems, those of the sort illustrated by the following example.

Example 4

Suppose that the distribution of heights of 20-year-old American men is known to be approximately normal and to have a mean of 5 feet 9 inches (i.e., 69 inches) and a standard deviation of 3 inches — in other words, N(69,3). What percentage of 20-year-old men are taller than 6 feet (i.e., 72 inches)?

We know from the 68%–95%–99.7% Rule that the heights of about 68% of the men will be within 3 inches (i.e., 1 standard deviation) of the mean, 69 inches. So 68% of the men will be from 66 inches to 72 inches tall. The remaining 32% will be either shorter than 66 inches or taller than 72 inches. Because a normal distribution is symmetric, half of the 32% (16%) must be shorter than 66 inches and the other half (the

---

7. You might want to compare these percentages to those in Chebychev's Rule, which, as you'll remember, applies to all distributions, not just to normal distributions.

other 16%) taller than 72 inches. Thus, the answer to the question is 16%.

E. Z Scores and the Z Table

The preceding example was relatively easy to work through because the difference between the mean (69 inches) and the value of interest (72 inches) was exactly 1 standard deviation (3 inches). In the vast majority of real-life situations, however, the difference between the two values doesn't translate into a whole number of standard deviations. In such cases, while an approximate answer can be derived using the 68%-95%-99.7% Rule, a much more exact answer can be obtained using z scores and a z table.

How to . . .

> **. . . calculate a z score**
> 1. Subtract the mean of the distribution from any given value to get a deviation score.
> 2. Divide the deviation by the standard deviation of the distribution. The result is the z score for the given value.

A z score tells how far, as measured in standard deviations, any given value is from the mean of a distribution. It also tells whether the value is larger than or smaller than the mean: the value is larger than the mean if the z score is positive and smaller if the z score is negative.

Let's work through an example.

Example 5

> What is the z score for a height of 72 inches in the distribution described in the previous example?
> 1. We subtract 69 inches (the mean) from 72 inches (the height that we're interested in) and find that the difference (the deviation score) is 3 inches.
> 2. The next step is to divide 3 inches (the deviation) by 3 inches (the standard deviation score). The result is 1.0. So z = 1.0 for a height of 72 inches. In other words, a height of

72 inches is exactly 1 standard deviation larger than the mean height of 69 inches.

What if we wanted to know the percentage of 20-year-old American men who are taller than 74 inches? Figuring out the z score is simple enough: $(74 - 69)/3 = 1.67$. But how do we use this number? To solve this problem, we need to use the z-table (see Z-Table on page 105). The z-table provides, for any given z-score, the proportion of individuals in a normal distribution who would be expected to have a z-score *less* than the given z-score.

Example 6

Given the distribution of heights from Example 4, to find the percentage of 20-year-old American men who are taller than 74 inches, using the z table (see Z-Table on page 105)

1. We calculate the z score (we've already done this) and find that it's 1.67.

2. We find 1.6 (the z score through its first decimal place) in the far-left column of the z table (see Z-Table on page 105).

3. We move across the row that 1.6 is on until we reach the column labeled .07 (the second decimal place of the z score) at the top.

4. The number in the cell where the row and the column for our z score of 1.67 intersect, .9525, gives us the proportion of 20-year-old American men who would be expected to have a height the z-score of which is less than 1.67, i.e. the proportion of men who are shorter than 74 inches.

5. We convert the proportion, .9525, to a percentage by moving the decimal two places to the right, and we get 95.25%. Thus, 95.25% of 20-year-old American men are 74 inches or shorter.

6. If 95.25% are 74 inches or shorter, then the remainder, 4.75% (i.e., 100.00% − 95.25% = 4.75%), of 20-year-old American men are taller than 74 inches. And this is the answer to our question.

This is one way in which z scores can be used. We'll revisit them, as well as the normality assumption, a little later in the chapter.

2. One-Variable Inferential Statistics

One-variable inferential statistics is the science of using data derived from a relatively small number of individuals to make educated guesses about some characteristic of a larger group from which the individuals were selected. The smaller group is called a *sample*, the larger group is called a *population*, and the manner in which the smaller group was selected is referred to as the sampling method. Sampling is done in the service of the two fundamental procedures of inferential statistics: hypothesis testing and estimation. We'll cover both of these topics, but before we do, we

---

Box 3
The U.S. Census and Sampling

The Supreme Court was called on to decide for the census of 2000 whether the Constitution requires a census or whether sampling is permissible. Residents uncounted in the decennial census aren't randomly distributed throughout society. Rather, certain minorities, immigrants, and the poor — individuals from groups that traditionally are overwhelmingly Democratic — are disproportionately missed. Perhaps not surprisingly, Democrats favor sampling as a means to account for such individuals, because the population count affects Congressional districting and undercounting may result in less representation and funding for the undercounted groups. Republicans oppose sampling, arguing that it's unconstitutional. In fact, the only U.S. census that consisted of a head-by-head count was the first one — in 1790. Mail surveys have had a declining response rate over time, down from 78% in 1970 to 65% in 1990 alone. And it appears that the rate for the 2000 census will prove to be even lower. Statisticians are nearly universal in their support of sampling as a method for arriving at a count of the population that's closer to the true number than is possible through mail surveys.

should focus a little more closely on samples and sampling and touch on the issue of validity in relation to sample data.

A. Samples and Sampling

A data set may contain scores on one or more variables for *all* of the individuals — that is, the entire population — the researcher is interested in studying. Such a data set is a *census*. For example, a company's employment records contain a census of its employees' salaries, and a university registrar's office contains a census of student grades. Though the U.S. census aspires to be a true census, it doesn't achieve this goal. (See box 3.)

Often, however, gathering complete information isn't a viable option. The task may be prohibitively expensive (e.g., a pollster would like to know what *all* Americans think of lawyers but can afford to ask only 500 or 1,000 people), practically impossible (e.g., a pharmaceutical company would like to know what would happen if everyone with a stomach ulcer were treated with a new drug that it is developing), or truly impossible (e.g., a stock market analyst would like to know at what level the S&P 500 stock index will be for each of the next twenty weeks). In such situations, the best the researcher can do is measure the variable of interest for some sample of the population under investigation and, by applying techniques of statistical inference to the resulting measurements, try to make educated guesses about what the measurements on all the other individuals in the population would be if they were actually collected.

The distinction between sample and population is crucial to inferential statistics. To help maintain the distinction, statisticians call true numerical descriptors of populations *parameters* and the numerical descriptors of samples used to estimate parameters *statistics*. For instance, population mean (μ), population variance (σ^2), and population standard deviation (σ) are parameters, whereas sample mean ($\bar{x}$), sample variance (s^2), and sample standard deviation (s) are statistics. The goal of sampling is to select a sample sufficiently representative of the population that statistics derived from it provide accurate estimations of the population parameters.

Because a sample is intended to represent a population, for it to work well in statistical inference, it must be typical of the population with respect to the variable being studied. For any variable, the degree to which the sample distribution resembles the population distribution is the *representativeness of the sample*. Analysts and researchers can't search through the population to find perfectly typical subsets of individuals, so they rely on randomization to produce an approximately representative sample. A *simple random sample* is one that's selected in such a way that it was no more and no less likely to be selected than was any other possible sample of the same size — in other words, all possible samples of the given size had the same likelihood of being selected. Note that this is not the same thing as a sample in which each *individual* has the same chance of being selected. (Do you see the difference?) Randomization can be achieved in a variety of ways, ranging from drawing slips of paper from a box containing one slip for each member of the population (a method suitable for sampling from small populations) to using random number generating computer programs. All sound methods do, however, have something in common: their starting point, which is always a carefully constructed definition of the relevant population.

Randomization doesn't guarantee representativeness. It does, however, allow analysts to control for bias and apply statistical techniques to the data collected. If a sample isn't random (or at least approximately so), it isn't appropriate for use in making statistical inferences about the underlying population.

To avoid the expense involved in random sampling, many social science studies gather data from *convenience samples*. These are samples that comprise individuals who have been chosen because they were relatively accessible. For example, college students enrolled in psychology courses account for the majority of individuals in samples used for psychology experiments. The researchers who rely on such samples would like to claim that they learn facts, not simply about the nature of college students, but about general human nature. Whether an inference of this kind is justified depends on the answer to the question: With respect to the variable being investigated, how representative of the population of all humans are college students enrolled in psychology courses? And this is a question to be answered by informal argument, not by application of statistical techniques.

Consider the following examples. Are the sampling methods described likely to yield truly representative samples of the populations of interest?

- To determine whether her constituents favor a proposed gun-control bill, a Congresswoman tallies the views expressed in letters from her constituents.

- To determine the percentage of motorists who drive while under the influence of alcohol, the state police administer a Breathalyzer test to the driver of every twentieth car passing a highway checkpoint.

- To determine what a town's residents would be willing to pay to preserve the local environment, a company interested in building a chemical factory near the town surveys the shoppers at a nearby Wal-Mart.

- The Student Life Committee at Legal Eagle Law School would like to know how important the opportunity to travel is to students' choice of future employment. The committee polls the law students taking a class in international trade at the school.

- To select a jury pool, county officials call the home phone numbers of randomly selected registered voters between 12:00 noon and 5:00 P.M. on weekdays (Mondays through Fridays) and summon any eligible adult who answers.

- To determine how many apples in a crate are rotten, a grocer inspects the ones at the top of the crate.

B. Survey Data and Validity

If the results of statistical inference are to be sound, not only must the sampling technique be proper, but the measurements of the variable in question must be valid as well. *Validity* is the extent to which a measuring instrument measures what it's intended to measure. (Is a polygraph a valid device for detecting lying? Is the LSAT a valid test of aptitude for law school? Does your bathroom scale produce an accurate measure of your weight?) If the data on which we base our statistical inferences are invalid, then we'll be unable to accurately generalize about population characteristics. Validity is a particularly acute problem in *survey design,* because there often are good reasons to suspect that survey responses don't reflect the true views of respondents.

Although much of the data that appear in law and public policy settings are derived from surveys, the study of valid survey design has remained relatively undeveloped. Most surveys are designed to be *face valid.* That is, they consist of questions that request directly and obviously the information desired (e.g., How old are you? What was your income last year? How happy are you at law school? Who do you intend to vote for in the upcoming presidential election?). The responses are compiled, and the results from the samples are offered as truths about the age, income, level of satisfaction, and voting proclivities of the respective populations. The designers of face-valid surveys often ignore well-established truths about the complexity of the relationship between what people report their beliefs, attitudes, and behaviors to be when they participate in surveys and what their beliefs, attitudes, and behaviors actually are. Yet accepting the accuracy of sampling (routinely reported as a margin of error — e.g., a margin of error of ±3 percentage points — when the survey results are presented) as a measure of the validity of survey results is commonplace.

The validity problem is obvious with some survey questions (e.g., How often have you used the following substances in the past month: cocaine, heroin, PCP?). But even relatively innocuous questions (e.g., How old are you? What was your income last year?) are unlikely, for a variety of reasons, to yield completely reliable data. Sometimes, for example, all it takes is a small alteration in wording to bring about a major change in the distribution of responses to a question. Compare (1) with (2) : (1) Do you think the United States should forbid public speeches against democracy? (2) Do you think the United States should allow public speeches against democracy? You might think that a *yes* answer to the first is equivalent to a *no* answer to the second, but in the survey from which these questions were taken, only 20% of respondents answered *yes* to the first question whereas 45% of respondents answered *no* to the second question. Indeed, polls regularly find much less public support for "a constitutional amendment prohibiting abortion" than they do for "a constitutional amendment protecting the life of an unborn child."

Sophisticated survey designers are well aware of such problems, however, it's often in the interest of the party sponsoring a survey for a question to be posed in a form that produces less valid responses. Compare, for example, two questions designed to obtain information about the pervasiveness of harassment at law firms: (1) Have you ever observed or do you know of anyone else who has ever observed an incident of harassment at your law firm? (2) Have you been harassed at your law firm? Which is likely to be the question of choice for an interest group committed to combatting harassment?

A key point to remember in interpreting survey data is that people who take part in surveys aren't simply tools of the surveyor, single-mindedly committed to following instructions and providing useful data. Rather, they come with concerns of their own, which are often in tension with the goals of the survey designer. The *resulting motivational bias* is a serious threat to the validity of survey work. Some survey participants may, for example, be set on presenting a positive image (or at least not a negative image) of themselves. Think about how valid their responses would be to these questions: How many times per month do you watch X-rated movies? How often do you attend religious services? Other survey participants may want to further their own personal or political goals. Imagine tax lawyers polled about their views of the social desirability of simplifying the tax code, or doctors polled about the social desirability of caps on malpractice liability.[8] The result is likely to be seriously biased responses.

The way in which survey questions are put to participants can also introduce bias or exacerbate biases arising from other causes. Imagine, for example, a survey conducted face to face in which an attractive interviewer poses questions that require the participant to provide potentially embarrassing information.

Even data collected from respondents who have the intention of cooperating fully with the surveyor can be biased for any of a number of reasons. For example, respondents may discern from the way a question is worded (e.g., Do you believe that the Salvation Army should receive additional funding to continue its good works?) what sort of answer the survey designer is hoping to get, and often they are all too happy to oblige. Bias that arises in this way has been dubbed *acquiescence bias*.

---

8. In some instances, survey participants' opposing goals are very specific. This may be the case, for example, when potential jurors for a high-profile case, many of whom will have a strong, unexpressed desire to sit on the jury, fill out juror questionnaires. Similar tensions arise when people complete employment or mental health questionnaires.

Box 4
Sampling Validity

National Survey Finds Adultery Less
Common among Married Americans Than
Previously Thought

A national survey of American sexual practices has revealed that only 7% of married Americans have committed adultery within the past five years (margin of error ±2%). Previous estimates had ranged from 20% to 40%.

The above is based on press coverage of a widely reported academic study conducted in the 1990s. Some (though very few) newspapers did go on to reveal that this finding was derived from the frequency of yes and no responses to the question — Have you committed adultery within the past five years? — that an interviewer posed to all married respondents in their homes and in the presence of their spouses. Is this a valid measure of the frequency of adultery? (The cited margin of error, ±2 percentage points, is *not* an indication that the actual rate of adultery was between 5% and 9%. Rather, it's a measure of *sampling error* — an indication that, based on the sample results, had the entire population of married people been asked the same question under the same circumstances, it's very likely that between 5% and 9% would have answered yes.)

Although the way in which the question about adultery was put to survey participants may seem like an extreme example of surveyor insensitivity, consider the following: A prominent AIDS researcher reported that gay men who are infected with HIV are unlikely to know it. He based this claim on a survey of gay men done at popular gay nightclubs. Each was asked his HIV status, and gave a sample of blood. After pairing the survey responses and the results of the blood tests, the researcher calculated the percentage of HIV-infected respondents who had correctly identified themselves as HIV positive. Can you offer an alternative explanation for the results of this investigation?

Motivational and acquiescence biases can be very difficult to detect and control for. For this important reason (among others), people who do serious survey research conduct pilot studies — preliminary studies in which the planned survey instrument is administered to a small sample of respondents who are then individually interviewed at length about what the experience was like. Using this information, the designers can then revise their survey questions. Another important reason for conducting pilot studies is to uncover questions that could cause cognitive difficulties for the respondents. Perhaps some questions could be perceived as being vague. Maybe some contain unfamiliar words. Yet others might be difficult or impossible for respondents to answer because of the type or nature of the information requested (e.g., On average, how many hours per week do your children watch television? Over the past six months, what have you seen on television or read in the newspaper about tobacco litigation?).

Although survey data are routinely prone to serious sampling and validity problems, they're often the only sort of data available on a host of important public and private questions. Indeed, our democratic system itself requires surveys in the form of elections whereby a nonrandom sample of the population selects those who will govern the nation. Every major election in the United States is flawed by substantial sampling errors, validity problems, or both. But what alternatives do we have for eliciting information about the public will? Despite their serious shortcomings, surveys will persist into the foreseeable future as a major source of social data.

C. Hypothesis Testing

Now that we've explored, a little, where data come from, let's see how they're used in statistical inference. Consider the following scenario:

John and Mary, two law students, are discussing the cost of living in Lawville. Mary claims that the average rent paid by local law students is $950 a month. (Though John's probably correct in assuming that Mary's use of 'average' refers to the mean rent, he perhaps should have her verify that she isn't referring to the median rent.) Since he is currently taking a statistics course, John decides to test Mary's claim by surveying 100 of their fellow students, sampled randomly, about the rent they pay. The resulting sample of 100 rents has a mean of $1,000 and a standard deviation of $150. Data in hand, he approaches Mary.

JOHN: Sorry, Mary, but my survey shows you are wrong about the average rent.

MARY: (After looking at the results) No it doesn't, $1,000.00 is pretty close to $950.00, so you don't have any good evidence that I'm wrong. After all, if I flip a coin 20 times, I might expect to get, on average, 10 heads and 10 tails. But I wouldn't be surprised if I got 8 heads and 12 tails or, for that matter, 13 heads and 7 tails. And I certainly wouldn't decide on the basis of such outcomes that heads and tails weren't equally likely. So your experiment doesn't shake my belief that the real mean rent is $950.

JOHN: But what would you say if you got 19 heads and 1 tail? Or 1 head and 19 tails? You'd be pretty likely to conclude that the coin wasn't evenly balanced, wouldn't you? If you were right about the mean rent and it actually is $950, the chance is less than 1 in 2,500 that I would have come up with a sample with a mean of $1,000. So I think that your hypothesis is false.

This example illustrates the basic logic underlying statistical hypothesis testing. We begin with a claim — a hypothesis — about a population mean (i.e., that it has some particular value).[9] We select a random sample from the relevant population and calculate its mean. If the sample mean is so different from the hypothesized population mean that it's highly unlikely that we would have obtained such a sample value if the hypothesis had, indeed, been true, then we conclude that we have good evidence against the hypothesis. On the other hand, if the sample mean doesn't seem particularly unlikely, even though it differs from the hypothesized population mean, all we can conclude is that we don't have good evidence that the hypothesis is false.

So how did John conclude that the chance was less than 1 in 2,500 that his sample would have had a mean of $1,000 or more if Mary's claim (that the mean rent of the population of all student rents is $950) had been correct? He calculated a z score from his data and looked it up in the z table we used earlier in the chapter. Because John's z score was based on the mean of a sample consisting of 100 observations (i.e., n = 100) rather than on a single observation (in effect, a sample for which n = 1), as ours was in the earlier example, he had to use a formula a little more complicated than the one we used earlier. (For the moment, you'll have to accept on faith that this is the appropriate one.)

$$z = \frac{\bar{x} - \mu}{\sigma / \sqrt{n}}$$

Don't let this formula put you off. The numerator is just the difference between the sample mean ($\bar{x}$ = $1,000) and the hypothetical population mean (μ = $950). The denominator is the population standard deviation (for which, as John was taught, the sample standard deviation, s, may be substituted, so he could say σ = $150) divided by the square root of the sample size ($\sqrt{n} = \sqrt{100} = 10$).

---

9. There are methods for testing claims about the median and the standard deviation — indeed, any population parameter — but the mean is, by far, the one that's tested most often.

So,

$$z = \frac{\$1,000 - \$950}{\$150/10}$$
$$= \frac{\$50}{\$15}$$
$$= 3.33$$

The next step is for John to determine, using the z table, how un-likely it would be for him to randomly get a result with a z-score as large as 3.33. John looked up 3.33 in the z table. He found that the table entry corresponding to a z score of 3.33 is 0.9996, which is equivalent to 99.96%. This means that about 99.96% of the time, he could expect the sample mean to be less than 3.33 standard deviations above the population mean. Conversely, the chance that the z-score for a randomly chosen sample would be 3.33 or more was about 0.04% (i.e., 100.00% − 99.96% = 0.04%), or about 1 in 2,500. Given the extreme unlikelihood of his getting such a large sample mean if Mary were correct about the actual mean rent, John rejects Mary's hypothesis.

The hypothesis being tested is often referred to as the *null hypothesis*. The reason for this choice of language is the frequent use of hypothesis testing in the following kind of scientific situation: *A drug company researcher, Dr. Johnson, creates a new ointment which she has reason to believe will lessen the time it takes for minor cuts to heal. The company has data on the average time of healing of a standard cut — 52 hours with a standard deviation of 7 hours. To test the ointment, Dr. Johnson applies it to cuts newly inflicted on a group of volunteers. Their cuts heal on average in 50 hours. Is this good evidence that the ointment is effective? The null hypothesis is that the ointment is ineffective, i.e., that the population mean for cuts treated with the new ointment is not different from the population mean for cuts allowed to heal on their own.*

Often, in science the goal of an experiment is to see if some new treatment or drug or intervention makes a difference. If it does, that's a scientific discovery, and results in fame and fortune, or

---

Box 5
Z Scores with Percentages

In many legal contexts — notably in cases concerning allegations of discriminatory treatment — the question arises as to whether a group of employees or voters or jurors reflects the demographic characteristics of the population as a whole. Consider, for example, the case of Castaneda v. Partida, 430 U.S. 482 (1976). The criminal defendant alleged that Mexican-Americans were underrepresented on grand juries in Hidalgo County, Texas, where he was convicted of burglary with intent to rape. The county's population was 79% Mexican-American, but of the 870 residents summoned for jury duty, only 339 (i.e., 39%) were Mexican-American. How likely would such a large disparity be if the jury pool had been drawn randomly from the population (i.e., had been a true random sample of the population) of Hidalgo County?

We can use the Z test to answer this question, but because the data is given in percentages, we calculate Z using a formula that looks somewhat different from the one we used earlier:

$$z = \frac{\hat{p} - p}{\sqrt{p(1-p)}/\sqrt{n}}$$

where $\hat{p}$ is the sample percentage converted to its decimal equivalent (e.g., the percentage of Mexican-Americans in the sample of jurors, 39%, converted to 0.39), p is the population percentage converted to a decimal (e.g., the percentage of Mexican-Americans in the population of Hidalgo County, 79%, converted to 0.79), and n is the sample size (e.g., the number of jurors in the sample, 870). Using this formula, what is your answer to the question posed above?

---

at least, a publication for the scientist. If the treatment doesn't make a difference — cuts don't heal faster, patients don't live longer, etc. — then in the typical case, that's not news and no fame, fortune, or even publication results. The natural way for statisticians to approach the question of whether some intervention makes a difference is to use data to test the hypothesis that there is *no* difference (the null hypothesis) and to decide there probably *is* a difference if the null hypothesis is shown to be very unlikely. So, the scientist is usually eager to find a large enough difference between the background level and the sample result with the proposed treatment to be able to claim that there is very good evidence against the null hypothesis of no difference. A difference large enough to allow the scientist to make this latter claim is called a *statistically significant difference.*

A *statistically significant difference* between a population mean and the mean of a random sample is a difference large enough to justify the claim that the sample was taken from a population with a mean different from the mean of the given population. But just how large does a difference have to be in order to be statistically significant? It depends. The most common standard used by a majority of scientific journals (and courts) requires that the difference be large enough that it would have occurred by chance only 5% of the time or less if the null hypothesis (that there is no difference) were in fact true. When this standard of significance is met, the result is said to be significant at the 0.05 level or, equivalently, that the null hypothesis is *rejected at the 5% level of significance.* If you check the z table, you'll see that the 0.05 level of significance corresponds to a z less than – 1.96 or greater than 1.96. (Remember that setting the standard of statistical significance at .05 means that we have chosen to reject the null hypothesis if we observe a sample mean which is so far from the mean stated in the null hypothesis that we get such a sample mean less than 5% of the time when the null hypothesis is true.)

It's important to realize that nothing in the definition of statistical significance singles out 0.05 as *the* level that must be met for the null hypothesis to be rejected. Indeed, such a one-size-fits-all approach has come under increasing fire lately. As some scientists and statisticians have pointed out, a decision to reject the null hypothesis is a practical one: the null hypothesis should be rejected only if the data meet a standard that makes sense in terms of the nature and circumstances of the issue at hand, and the appropriate cutoff between significant and nonsignificant is the significance level corresponding to this standard.[10]

1. Type I and Type II errors. When you test a hypothesis there are four possible outcomes that can result from your test (see Figure 13). Boxes A and D show accurate test results. In A, we do not reject the null hypothesis when it is in fact true, and in D we reject the null hypothesis when it is in fact false. In B and C, however, our hypothesis test leads us to make an error. In C we fail to reject a false null hypothesis and in B we *do* reject a true null hypothesis. The sort of error made in B is called a Type I error. In Dr. Johnson's experiments this would be concluding that the salve is effective when it isn't. The sort of error made in C is called a Type II error. For Dr. Johnson, this would be concluding that she has insufficient evidence that the salve is effective when in fact it *is* effective. (Now would be a good time for you to identify the Type I and Type II errors in the rent example.)

For Dr. Johnson's drug company, a Type I error would result in beginning product development on an ineffective salve while a Type II error would result in missing the chance to develop an effective product. Which sort of error is of greater consequence to the drug company? Suppose that it is very costly for them to begin development of a new product and that ultimately if a product is ineffective that product cannot be marketed. In such a case the company would want to set standards for its product testing that will make Type I errors rare. Unfortunately, setting the standard of statistical significance in such a way as to make Type I errors more unlikely necessarily increases the risk of committing

---

10. In some contexts, researchers prefer to report a specific probability (p) of getting a particular result rather than a significance level at which the null hypothesis can be rejected: for example, *p = 0.016* rather than *significant at the 0.05 level*. This allows the consumer of the data to decide the significance of the question.

Figure 13
Hypothesis Testing: Possible Outcomes

Null hypothesis

	True	False
Do not reject null hypothesis	**A** Null is true. Test says do not reject.	**C** Null is false. Test says do not reject.
Reject null hypothesis	**B** Null is true. Test says reject.	**D** Null is false. Test says reject.

Result of hypothesis testing

Type II errors and vice versa. (Do you see why this must be true?)

In a criminal trial, the null hypothesis is "defendant is innocent." Rejecting a true null hypothesis (e.g. finding guilty when innocent) is a Type I error. Failing to reject a null hypothesis that is in fact false (e.g. finding innocent when guilty) is a Type II error. A crucial question for criminal procedure is where we should set the balance between these two types of errors.

FDA regulation of drugs also requires a balancing of Type I and Type II errors. The agency places substantial weight on avoiding Type II errors (wrongly approving unsafe drugs) and less emphasis on Type I errors (failing to approve safe and effective drugs). Should the FDA attempt to minimize Type II errors, given the resulting increase in Type I errors? Are there incentives operating on FDA employees that would explain their favoring the avoidance of Type II errors?

2. Sampling distributions and hypothesis testing.

It's the day after John's exchange with Mary. John arrives at his statistics class, pleased with himself for having so successfully put into practice what he's been learning.

JOHN: I used the right formula, didn't I?

INSTRUCTOR: Yes, you did, but do you know *why* it was the correct formula?

JOHN: Well . . . uh . . . uh . . . well . . . I guess I'm not exactly sure. But, as long as it's right . . .

INSTRUCTOR: This is a law school, not an engineering school. Our goal here is to *understand* statistics, not merely to gain technical proficiency. To help ensure that you and your 49 classmates understand inferential statistics, I'm going to have everyone in the class replicate your experiment. Each student in the class will select a sample of 100 students from the law school, ask them what they pay in rent, calculate the mean rent for their sample, and bring the result to class next week.

In class the following week, the instructor collects from the students the means of the 50 samples. He constructs one histogram from the 50 means and another from John's original data, the rents paid by the 100 students in John's sample (see Figure 14).

INSTRUCTOR: Take a look at the two histograms. What can you say about the relationship between the two distributions that they picture?

Figure 14
What Was on the Blackboard

Histogram of 50 Means

Histogram of John's Original Data of Rents Paid

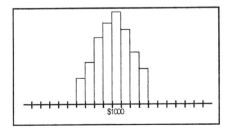
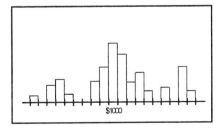

A STUDENT: Well, judging from the histograms, the means
of the two distributions are about the same, but
the distribution for the histogram on the right is
a lot more spread out than the one for the histogram on left. And the distribution for the
histogram on the left is pretty close to a normal
distribution.

INSTRUCTOR: You're exactly right. And it isn't by accident that
the two distributions have the characteristics you
mentioned. Rather, it's a consequence of the
most famous theorem in statistics: the *central
limit theorem.* Here is what it says:

> If you plot the means of a number of random
> samples of size n from a given population, you
> will notice three things: (1) the larger the n, the
> more closely the distribution of sample means
> will resemble a normal distribution (2) the mean
> of the distribution of sample means will be ap-
> proximately equal to the population mean (i.e.,
> μ), and (3) the standard deviation of the distri-
> bution of sample means will be approximately
> equal to the population standard deviation di-
> vided by the square root of the sample size (i.e.,
> $\sigma/\sqrt{n}$). In sum, the distribution of the means of
> random samples from a given population ap-
> proximates a normal distribution and has the
> same mean as the population from which the
> samples were drawn but a much smaller stan-
> dard deviation.

Let's briefly review the logic of hypothesis testing as applied to
John's experiment. The basic idea is that we select a sample, calculate its mean, and then determine our likelihood of having
selected a sample with that mean if our null hypothesis were true.
So the important question in John's experiment was: If, as Mary
hypothesized, the actual mean rent paid by law students is $950,

Box 6
The Central Limit Theorem in Action

Start with any distribution, regardless of the shape of its curve — say, the one represented by curve A (which is, obviously, very "non-normal"). Randomly pick samples of 5 values from the distribution, calculate the mean of the values, and plot the means. The graph of the resulting distribution, B, is narrower and more normal looking than that of the original distribution. Do the same for 10 values and, finally, for 30 values (or more), and you'll end up with distributions whose curves look like C and D, respectively. The sampling distribution for means of samples consisting of 30 values or more will be quite normal looking, whatever shape the curve of the initial distribution has.

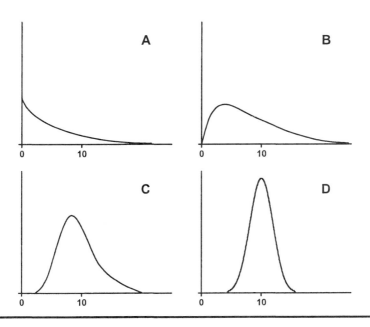

how likely would it be for any given random sample of 100 rents to have a mean of $1,000?

To answer this question, we begin by specifying what the distribution of means of samples of 100 rents would be like if Mary were correct (i.e., if the mean rent really were $950). Applying the central limit theorem, we know that the distribution would be approximately normal, that its mean would be $950, and that its standard deviation would be one-tenth of the standard deviation of the underlying population (i.e., $\sigma_{\text{sample means}} = \sigma_{\text{population}}/\sqrt{n} = \sigma_{\text{population}}/\sqrt{100} = \sigma_{\text{population}}/10$). See Figure 15 for a graphic representation of the sampling distribution (i.e., the distribution of sample means).

The next step is to determine the likelihood that any given random sample of 100 rents from that population would have a mean of $1,000. We can figure this out by calculating a z score for $1,000 (the data point in question) and using the z table to find out where in the distribution of sample means the $1,000 point falls. (If this procedure reminds you of the way we solved the height problem earlier in the chapter, you're right on track.) As we saw earlier, the formula for calculating a z score is

$$z = \frac{\bar{x} - \mu}{\sigma/\sqrt{n}}$$

Figure 15
Idealized Distribution of Means of Samples of 100 Rents under Mary's Hypothesis

$\mu_{\text{hypothesized}} = \$950$

$\sigma_{\text{sample means}} = \sigma_{\text{population}}/10 = \$15$

Before we do the calculation, let's take a moment to consider the components of this formula. The numerator should be recognizable as the deviation of a data point (here, each data point is a mean of a sample of 100 rents) from a given population mean (here, the population of all samples of 100 rents). And the denominator should be recognizable as the formula for the standard deviation of a sampling distribution for samples of size n. So the formula just embodies the rules for calculating z scores that were set out earlier in the chapter.

Our data point of interest (the mean of John's sample), $\bar{x}$, has a value of $1,000. Our hypothesized mean (the figure that Mary claims to be the population mean), μ, is $950. The size of the samples from which the sampling distribution is derived, n, is 100. But we don't know the standard deviation of the population, σ, which we need to calculate the z score. Fortunately however, the sample standard deviation is acceptable as an estimate of the population standard deviation. So we can do what John did: substitute the standard deviation of his sample: $150 for σ. What we end up with is

$$z = \frac{\bar{x} - \mu}{\sigma/\sqrt{n}}$$
$$= \frac{\$1,000 - \$950}{\$150/10}$$
$$= \frac{\$50}{\$15}$$
$$= 3.33$$

The probability that any given sample of 100 will have a mean of $1,000 or more if the true population mean is $950 can be found by looking up this z score in the z table.

Note that using a z score to test a hypothesis requires that the *sampling distribution* (the distribution of sample means), be normal, though the distribution of the population from which the samples were drawn, need not be. According to the central limit theorem, if the samples are of adequate size — in practice, adequate size turns out to be at least 30 individuals or so — the distribution of their means is approximately normal. Hence, as long as samples are of sufficient size, using a z score to test a hypothesis is warranted.

This would be a good time for you to go back to the introduction to z scores and take another look at the example we worked through there (the one involving heights of 20-year-old American men). Can you see the basic similarity between comparing a single observation to a distribution of observations and comparing a single sample mean to a distribution of sample means?

D. Estimation

If you understand the material on hypothesis testing that we just covered, you're in a position to master *estimation,* the other basic technique of statistical inference. Estimation enables us to use sample data to make an educated guess about the mean of the population from which a sample was drawn.[12] Like hypothesis testing, estimation ultimately relies on the central limit theorem.

Suppose that John wanted to estimate from his sample data the mean rent paid by law students in Lawville. What would be his best guess? An obvious choice is $1,000, the mean of his sample. Indeed, this would be an acceptable estimate for most purposes, though it's very unlikely to be exactly right. (Why?) The sample mean provides a *point estimate* (so called because it's a single value — i.e., a point — in the entire spectrum of possible values) of the parameter. A point estimate by itself generally isn't as useful as an *interval estimate,* which specifies both a range of values and the probability that the true value of the parameter is somewhere within this range. John could, for example, use his data to calculate an interval such that the actual population mean will be between its upper and lower boundaries 95% of the time. Let's do this for him, solving the problem step by step.

---

12. Other parameters can be estimated, but the mean is estimated much more often than any of the others.

But first, because we'll be working with three different distributions, we should take a moment to make sure that we're clear on what they are and to establish some notation. The distributions are (1) the population of student rents, (2) the sampling distribution (i.e., the means of random samples of the population of student rents), and (3) John's own sample of student rents. The respective standard deviations will be designated $\sigma_{population}$, $\sigma_{sample\ means}$, and s_{John}.

According to the central limit theorem, the sampling distribution (i.e., the distribution of the means of sample rents), which is based on samples of 100, is approximately normal, and

$$\mu_{sample\ means} = \mu_{population}$$

and

$$\sigma_{sample\ means} = \frac{\sigma_{population}}{\sqrt{100}}$$

$$= \frac{\sigma_{population}}{10}$$

Because the sampling distribution is approximately normal, the 68-95-99% Rule tells us that about 95% of the means of all possible samples lie within 2 standard deviations of its mean ($\mu_{population} \pm 2\sigma_{sample\ means}$), as illustrated in Figure 16. Thus, the likeli-

Figure 16
Distribution of the Means of Samples of 100 Rents
from a Population of Rents with a Mean of μ
and a Standard Deviation of σ

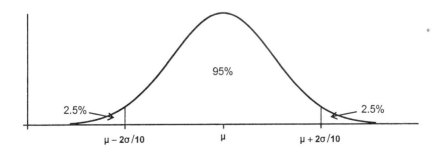

hood is 95% that the mean of John's sample ($\bar{x}_{John}$) — or that of any other sample of 100 rents — lies within this interval. (Do you understand why?) So $\bar{x}_{John}$ has a 95% chance of being within the interval $\mu_{population} \pm 2\sigma_{sample\ means}$.

To be able to define the boundaries of the interval, we have to know two parameters: $\mu_{population}$ and $\sigma_{sample\ means}$. As noted above, the mean of John's sample ($\bar{x}_{John}$, which is $1,000), is an acceptable estimate of $\mu_{population}$. But how can we estimate $\sigma_{sample\ means}$? We could calculate it from $\sigma_{population}$, but we don't know $\sigma_{population}$. We do, however, know the standard deviation of John's sample (s_{John}, which is $150), and it's an acceptable estimate of $\sigma_{population}$. Thus, we can, after all, calculate $\sigma_{sample\ means}$.

$$\sigma_{sample\ means} = \frac{\sigma_{population}}{\sqrt{100}}$$

$$= \frac{\sigma_{population}}{10}$$

$$= \frac{s_{John}}{10}$$

$$= \frac{\$150}{10}$$

$$= \$15$$

So

$$2\sigma_{sample\ means} = 2(\$15)$$

$$= \$30$$

and the lower boundary of the interval is

$$\mu_{population} - 2\sigma_{sample\ means} = \mu_{population} - \$30$$

$$= \bar{x}_{John} - \$30$$

$$= \$1,000 - \$30$$

$$= \$970$$

and the upper boundary is

$$\mu_{population} + 2\sigma_{sample\ means} = \mu_{population} + \$30$$
$$= \overline{x}_{John} + \$30$$
$$= \$1,000 + \$30$$
$$= \$1,030$$

Hence, there's a 95% probability that $\mu_{population}$ (the mean rent paid by law students in Lawville) is between $970 and $1,030. The $970–$1,030 interval is the 95% *confidence interval*.

How to . . .

> *. . . calculate a confidence interval for a population mean from sample data (n>30).*
>
> 1. Estimate the mean of the population by using the sample mean:
>
> $$\mu_{population} = \overline{x}$$
>
> 2. Calculate the standard deviation of the distribution of sample means for your sample size n
>
> $$\sigma_{sample\ means} = \frac{\sigma_{population}}{\sqrt{n}}$$
>
> (if the standard deviation of the population is known)
>
> or
>
> $$\sigma_{sample\ means} = \frac{s}{\sqrt{n}}$$
>
> (if the standard deviation of the population isn't known, as is usually the case)
>
> 3. Calculate the boundaries of the interval corresponding to the desired confidence level:
>
> a. For the 95% confidence interval, we would use the same formula as described above[13]:
>
> $$\overline{x} - 1.96\sigma_{sample\ means} \text{ and } \overline{x} + 1.96\sigma_{sample\ means}$$

---

13. In this example, we use the more precise 1.96 coefficient, which comes from the z table, rather than the rounded-off 2.0 coefficient used earlier.

b. More generally, the confidence interval is the range of values between

$$\overline{x} - (z \text{ score} \times \sigma_{\text{sample means}}) \text{ and}$$
$$\overline{x} + (z \text{ score} \times \sigma_{\text{sample means}})$$

where z score is the z score corresponding to the desired confidence level.

(Using John's sample data, what would the 90% confidence interval be for the mean rent paid by law students?)

The material on estimation that we've just covered is difficult, so don't be concerned if you feel that you don't yet have a firm grip on it. The best way to master the concepts is by working through practice problems — and the more problems you tackle, the better your understanding will be.

E. Statistical Significance and the Real World

Before wrapping up, we should return for a final, brief visit to Legal Eagle Law School.

Mary and John are chatting as they head for the cafeteria.

MARY: So maybe I was wrong. But I wasn't far wrong.
             Who cares if I was off by $50 or so?

There is truth in Mary's comment, which illustrates an important point: a statistically significant difference doesn't necessarily have any practical significance. It may have little or no real-world importance even if it's statistically significant at a very high level. This is very commonly the case when the sample from which the data have been obtained is large. (Why? Hint: How does the standard deviation of a sampling distribution, $\sigma_{\text{sample means}}$, change when the size of the samples on which it's based, n, increases?)

In some fields, though, very small differences, even 0.1%, can be of enormous significance, and it's extremely important to be certain that the differences are real. This is the case, for example, when two treatments for a widespread illness are compared. Let's

Box 7
Potential Pitfalls in Hypothesis Testing

Suppose that Mello, a soft-drink company, wants "scientific evidence" that consumers prefer its new lemon-lime soft drink to the lemon-lime drink of a rival company. And suppose that the new drink has been formulated so as to taste exactly like its competitor. Mello hires twenty independent researchers who are unknown to each other. Each researcher conducts taste tests in which randomly chosen consumers taste the two drinks from unlabeled glasses and are rewarded with a six-pack of the soft drink they like better. When Mello receives the results of the twenty experiments, it shreds nineteen of the reports and keeps one, which it claims offers "scientific evidence" at the 0.05 level of significance, that consumers prefer its new soft drink to that of the rival company. Given that the retained study does, in fact, conclude at the 0.05 level of significance that consumers prefer Mello's lemon-lime drink, is the company's claim consistent with what you know of the logic of hypothesis testing?

A more troubling version of this problem routinely occurs in well-established areas of scientific research. Because scientific journals, almost without exception, will publish only research that finds "significant" differences, studies that don't reject the null hypothesis are often filed away, never to see the light of day. Suppose that 100 researchers in different parts of the world, unknown to each other, are studying whether an over-the-counter drug can cause birth defects in infants born to women who took the drug during pregnancy. Eventually, five papers on the effects of the drug are published in scientific journals. Given what you know of the practices of scientific journals, will these five papers together present an accurate view of the harmful effects of the drug? This problem, which is of serious concern to those who base arguments on published scientific research (including tort lawyers), has been dubbed the "file drawer problem."

A related problem is the "cancer cluster problem." States publish annually the incidence of each major type of cancer for each of their counties. Suppose that a state has 25 counties and that incidence data are listed for 10 types of cancer. A tort lawyer scans the list and observes that the incidence of liver cancer in one county is

---

Box 7 (cont.)
Potential Pitfalls in Hypothesis Testing

significantly above the statewide incidence (0.05 significance level). Is this good evidence that some unusual agent that causes liver cancer is at work in that county? What if the list had been a national list that provided incidence data for the same 10 types of cancer in 1,000 counties?

---

say that a certain kind of possibly fatal heart disease can be treated with treatment A or treatment B. And suppose further that a series of clinical trials produces statistically significant results suggesting that the survival rates associated with the two treatments are 67.2% and 67.3%. Although it might appear that the difference of 0.1% is unimportant, if 1 million people suffer from the type of heart disease in question, using the better treatment will save, on average, 1,000 lives a year.

3. Suggestions for Further Reading

G.M. Clarke and D. Cooke, *A Basic Course in Statistics,* 4th ed. (New York, Oxford University Press, 1998). A thorough introduction to statistics for the intelligent beginner.

Lawrence C. Hamilton, *Statistics with Stata,* Version 8. (Pacific Grove, Calif.: Duxbury Press, 2003). If you want to perform data analysis on your own, you will need a statistics software package. Stata is an excellent program for beginners.

David Hand, Heikki Mannila, and Padhraic Singth, *Principles of Data Mining* (Cambridge, Mass.: MIT Press, 2001). An excellent introduction to the statistical analysis of large data sets.

David Salsburg, *The Lady Tasting Tea — How Statistics Revolutionized Science in the Twentieth Century.* (New York: Henry Holt and Company 2001). A throughly engaging portrayal of the people and events responsible for the development of modern statistics.

Edward Tufte, *The Visual Display of Quantitative Information*, 2nd ed. (Boston: Graphics Press, 2002). A modern classic updated.

Herbert F. Weisberg, Jon A. Krosnick and Bruce D. Bowen, *An Introduction to Survey Research Polling, and Data Analysis.* (Thousand Oaks, CA: Sage Publications, 1996). A standard work on the design and analysis of surveys.

II

Multivariate Statistics

In Part I, we introduced some methods for performing the three fundamental tasks of statistical analysis — data description, hypothesis testing, and estimation — using one-variable data sets. Now the focus shifts to the analysis of multivariate data sets, i.e. data sets composed of values, or scores, on two or more variables for each of a set of individuals.

1. Bivariate Statistics

The simplest form of multivariate statistics — bivariate statistics — probes the relationship between just two variables. The data sets of interest consist of *paired values*, one score on each of two variables for every individual in the set. Important questions in many fields seem to be natural candidates for bivariate analysis: Do high LSAT scores indicate that students will do well in law school? Is smoking bad for your health? Do grade-school students learn better in smaller classes? Does wearing a seat belt decrease the chance of sustaining serious injuries in car wrecks? Are the prices of stocks with high P/E ratios likely to decline? Such questions arise when a party wants to be able to predict or manipulate a variable using information about its relation to some other variable with which it is associated.[1]

---

1. Although any combination of categorical or quantitative variables can be analyzed with bivariate methods, we'll consider here only situations where both variables are quantitative.

A. Scatterplots

The most common form of pictorial presentation of bivariate data sets is the scatterplot, a type of graph on which each individual's scores on both variables are plotted as a single point. The pattern created by the points in a scatterplot can reveal the nature of the relationship between the two variables.

The Starchway scenario presented in the preceding chapter provides a good example of a situation where a scatterplot may be a helpful way to analyze data. To refresh your memory, Mary Starchway is defending against a claim of gender discrimination in pay at her company, Starchway Cookies.

Example 1

> Ms. Starchway claims that the gender differential for wages at her company is a by-product of paying higher salaries to employees with more experience. (Indeed, a common defense in such cases is that the difference in pay is due, not to discrimination, but to innocent practices, such as tying salary to education level, giving a raise every year to all employees, and so forth.) To support her contention, she puts together a table, listing each employee's gender, salary, and number of years of relevant experience (see Table 1).[2] As a first step in evaluating Ms. Starchway's claim, we can construct a scatterplot from the data for the two quantitative variables — salary and relevant experience.

How to . . .

> *. . . construct a scatterplot*
> To construct a scatterplot for two quantitative variables measured on the same set of individuals:

---

2. Even though there are three variables in the data set, this can be considered a bivariate case, because our immediate concern is with only two of them (salary and experience). However, if we wanted to know whether gender has an impact on the relationship between salary and experience, we could plot salary against experience for males and females separately.

Table 1
Example 9-1: Gender, Salary, and Experience
of Starchway Employees

Employee	Gender	Salary ($000s)	Experience (no. of years)
1	m	25	2
2	m	50	4
3	f	40	4
4	m	75	5
5	f	40	7
6	f	50	13
7	f	20	1
8	m	50	4
9	m	50	4
10	f	70	15
11	m	25	1
12	f	20	2
13	f	250	6
14	m	100	9
15	m	75	6
16	m	50	5
17	f	20	1
18	f	50	3
19	m	100	7
20	f	40	5

  1. Label the x-axis of a graph with the name of one variable and its unit of measurement.

  2. Select an appropriate scale for the x-axis (a scale that allows the axis to accommodate all scores on the variable), and mark and label the axis accordingly.

  3. Do the same along the y-axis for the other variable.

  4. For each individual in the data set, place a mark at the point where a vertical line drawn through the value of the

Figure 1
Starchway Employees: Salary and Experience

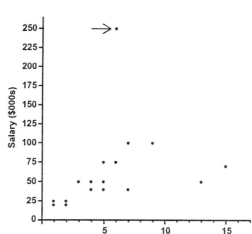

x-axis variable would intersect a horizontal line drawn through the value of the y-axis variable.

Applying these steps to the data in Table 1 gives us Figure 1. Does salary appear to go up as experience increases, as would be consistent with Ms. Starchway's claim? Well, it looks as if there may be such a tendency. However, several exceptions are clearly apparent. The two employees with the most experience do not by any means have the highest salaries. And the employee with the highest salary by far, has what looks to be only about average experience.

When analyzing scatterplots, statisticians bring to the task a mental set of ideal shapes, just as they do when approaching graphic presentations of single-variable data. The difference is that the entries in this second mental catalog represent ideal relationships between two variables rather than ideal distributions of one variable. The most important shape for describing scatterplots is, without a doubt, the straight line. When all the points in a scatterplot can be connected by a single straight line, we say the two variables plotted in the scatterplot have a perfect linear relationship. In practice, however, bivariate data virtually always fall short of perfect linearity, and statisticians have to decide, case by case, whether the relationship between the two variables is "linear enough" to treat it as linear.

B. Linear Relationships

As you may remember from math classes you've taken, every equation for a straight line has the simple form $y = a + bx$, where a and b are constants and x and y are variables, one plotted on the x-axis and the other on the y-axis. When two variables are linearly related, such an equation can be used to calculate y (the value of the variable represented along the y-axis) from any given x (the value of the variable represented along the x-axis) and vice versa. In the case of the two variables in Figure 2 (Fahrenheit temperature and Centigrade temperature), the linear equation is $°F = 32 + (9/5 × °C)$. Hence, for any given temperature in degrees Fahrenheit, we can calculate the equivalent temperature in degrees Centigrade, and for any given temperature in degrees Centigrade, we can calculate the equivalent temperature in degrees Fahrenheit. In other words, the relationship between Fahrenheit and Centigrade temperatures is one of complete predictability.

Figure 2
Temperature Scales: A Linear Relationship

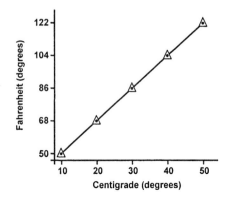

Centigrade (degrees)

Unfortunately, such perfect relationships are virtually always the result of a definitional connection, as is the case for the Fahrenheit and Centigrade temperature scales. When we construct scatterplots from actual data, what we see are generally much less tidy arrangements of points, such as those in Figure 3.

Though not perfectly linear, the relationships between the pairs of variables depicted in each of the scatterplots in Figure 3 can be

**Figure 3
Bivariate Data: Scatterplots**

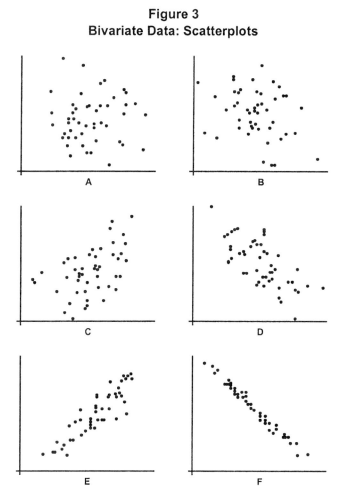

described as more or less linear, from scatterplot A which exhibits no apparent linear relationship, to scatterplot B reflecting a weak linear relationship, to scatterplots C and D representing moderately strong linear relationships, and finally to scatterplots E and F which portray strong linear relationships. When two variables have a strong linear relationship it means that there's a linear equation that will enable us to do a very good job of predicting the value of either variable from the corresponding value of the other variable. In contrast, when the linear relationship is weak or nonexistent, there is no linear equation that will be of much predictive use.

C. The Pearson Correlation Coefficient

Although the strength of the linearity of a relationship between two quantitative variables can be roughly estimated simply by inspecting a scatterplot, a precise measure, the Pearson correlation coefficient, is generally calculated. This coefficient, r, is a number between –1.0 and +1.0 that describes not only the strength of the linear relationship between two variables, but also its direction, positive or negative.

Variables may be correlated positively, negatively or not at all. Two variables are *positively correlated* if above-average values of one tend to accompany above-average values of the other, and below-average values of one tend to accompany below-average values of the other. Education and income, for example, are positively correlated. A correlation coefficient greater than 0 but less than or equal to +1.0 indicates that variables are positively correlated. Two variables are *negatively correlated* if below-average values of one tend to accompany above-average values of the other and vice versa. A country's mortality rate and its GNP, for example, are negatively correlated. A correlation coefficient less than 0 but greater than or equal to -1.0 signifies that variables are negatively correlated. The closer to +1.0, in the case of positive correlations or -1.0 in the case of negative correlation, the stronger the linear relationship is. A correlation coefficient of 0 or close to 0 indicates the absence of a linear relationship between the two variables.[3]

To get a feel for correlation coefficients, let's look at Figure 4. The scatterplots in this figure are the same as those in Figure 3, but now they're accompanied by their correlation coefficients. Note how our qualitative descriptions pair up with the correlation coefficients) of the depicted linear relationships (Table 2).

Table 2
Qualitative and Quantitative Descriptions of the
Scatterplots pictured in Figure 9-4

Scatterplot	Qualitative description	Quantitative description
A	none	$r = 0.00$
B	weak negative	$r = -0.30$
C	moderate positive	$r = 0.50$
D	moderate negative	$r = -0.70$
E	strong positive	$r = 0.90$
F	very strong negative	$r = -0.99$

Correlation coefficients must be interpreted with some degree of care, for they are subject to a number of distorting influences. For example, just like means of single-variable data sets, they can be profoundly affected by outliers. For a clear illustration of this phenomenon, let's look again at Figure 1: the correlation coeffi-

---

3. Because correlation coefficients are derived from sample values, the concerns pointed out in the previous chapter regarding the relationship between sample values and population values apply here as well. In particular, confidence intervals can be calculated for a correlation coefficient derived from sample data, and the hypothesis that two variables are correlated (i.e., that their correlation coefficient is different from 0) can be tested by using sample data. The methods for doing so are, however, beyond the scope of this book.

Figure 4
Bivariate Data: Correlation Coefficients

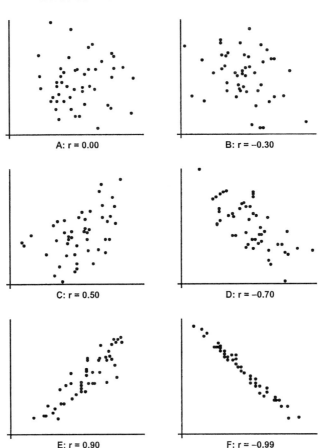

cient between experience and salary calculated from the data plotted there turns out to be 0.3289, which is far from the 0.6030 that's obtained if the data for the single (but extreme) outlying point are excluded from the calculation.

Considering all the talk about calculations of correlation coefficients, you're no doubt wondering *how* they're calculated.

How to . . .

. . . calculate the Pearson correlation coefficient

1. For a data set consisting of n individuals and two vari-

ables, X and Y, calculate the mean and standard deviation for each of the 2 variables

2. For each individual in the data set, calculate the z score for the value of variable X:

$$z_{X_1} = (X_1 - \bar{x})/s_X$$
$$z_{X_2} = (X_2 - \bar{x})/s_X$$
$$\ldots$$
$$z_{X_n} = (X_n - \bar{x})/s_X$$

3. For each individual, calculate the z score for the value of variable Y:

$$z_{Y_1} = (Y_1 - \bar{y})/s_Y$$
$$z_{Y_2} = (Y_2 - \bar{y})/s_Y$$
$$\ldots$$
$$z_{Y_n} = (Y_n - \bar{y})/s_Y$$

4. Multiply each individual's two z scores to get the product:

$$z_{X_1} \times z_{Y_1}$$
$$z_{X_2} \times z_{Y_2}$$
$$\ldots$$
$$z_{X_n} \times z_{Y_n}$$

5. Add the products of the z scores:

$$(z_{X_1} \times z_{Y_1}) + (z_{X_2} \times z_{Y_2}) + \ldots + (z_{X_n} \times z_{Y_n})$$

6. Divide the sum by n − 1 to arrive at the Pearson correlation coefficient:

$$r = \frac{(z_{X_1} \times z_{Y_1}) + (z_{X_2} \times z_{Y_2}) + \ldots + (z_{X_n} \times z_{Y_n})}{n - 1}$$

Quite obviously, calculating the correlation coefficient can be a messy affair for all but the smallest of data sets. Fortunately, computer programs now assume the burden. The task is manageable for small data sets, however, and working through the calculations by hand at least once can be very informative.

1. Correlation and causation. It can be very tempting to think of correlation as an indicator of causation. After all, why would the value of one variable increase — or, for that matter, decrease —

in direct proportion to an increase in the value of another variable unless some causal mechanism were at work? When a bicyclist pedals faster, for example, her heart rate increases, and when the demand for gasoline rises, consumers are charged more for it. On the other hand, when the supply of air conditioners decreases, their price goes up, and when the number of people using seatbelts increases, the number of highway fatalities goes down. In all these instances, it's plausible to think that a change in the value of one variable is responsible for — causes — the change in the other.

A few moments of reflection, however, is probably all that's required for you to realize that a correlation between two variables, even a very strong correlation, doesn't necessarily mean that a change in one of the variables causes the corresponding change in the other variable. Consider, for example, LSAT scores and first-year law school grades. Although there's a modest to moderate correlation between them, it's certainly not true that scoring high on the LSAT *causes* a law student to get high grades in the first year of law school. More plausibly, a third variable — probably some sort of ability that enables people to do well (or poorly) on the LSAT as well as on first-year exams — accounts for the correlation. In the same vein, hand size and foot size are highly correlated, though surely not because bigger hands cause bigger feet or vice versa but because some of the genes that influence the size of one also influence the size of the other. Situations like these illustrate what is known as the common response problem.

Box 1
Correlation: Some Illustrations

College grades and first-year law school grades	<0.30
LSAT scores and first-year law school grades	~0.40
Heights of fraternal twins	~0.50
Heights of identical twins	~0.95

Sometimes even though a causal relationship between two correlated variables exists its strength may be difficult to estimate because one or more other unaccounted for variables are also contributing to the correlation. The length of one's rap sheet, for example, is negatively correlated with one's yearly salary. But are these variables correlated because employers are prejudiced against hiring repeat offenders? Or because the time repeat offenders spend committing crimes or serving sentences cuts into the time they can devote to education or employment? Or because the character of career criminals isn't compatible with success in high-paying jobs? Clearly, it's a mistake to infer that the strength of the causal relationship between rap-sheet length and yearly salary is similar to the strength of their correlation.

When a correlation coefficient misleads as to the strength of a causal connection between two correlated variables because it reflects not only the relationship between those variables but also the influence of one or more other variables whose individual effects can't easily be isolated and assessed, there is said to be *confounding*. More generally, confounding is said to occur whenever a causal inference based on a data set is determined to be ill-founded because of the operation of a variable or variables which are not in the original data set. And the unaccounted for variables are variously referred to as confounders, or lurking variables.

Here's another example of confounding: for high schools in the United States, average teacher's salary and average student SAT score are moderately to highly correlated. Will paying teachers more result in improved student SAT scores? What are some potential confounders that might explain the apparent strength of this relationship?

Confounders are widely prevalent, and they have the potential to lead the unwary astray. But you'll avoid falling into the trap if you let this maxim be your guide: correlation doesn't imply causation; even a very strong correlation between two variables isn't in and of itself conclusive evidence that a change in one causes a change in the other. The implication is that you shouldn't rely solely on correlational analysis if you want to investigate causal relationships between variables.

The field of experimental methodology is concerned largely with the making of sound causal inferences from controlled observations. Most of the time, however, the data encountered in law and social policy making haven't been derived from experiments. When causation is a critical issue — and you don't have experimental evidence — you must do the best that you can with existing data sets. Commonly, this will involve gathering data on many variables and looking for patterns in the correlations among them. Further analysis will require the use of multiple regression (which will be addressed a little later) or some other statistical method appropriate for multivariate data analysis.

Just as correlation doesn't imply causation, causation doesn't imply correlation. Correlation reflects a linear relationship. If the association between two variables is nonlinear, the correlation coefficient may be small, even though the relationship is quite strong. The data from psychological research on motivation and performance provide what has become a famous example of this phenomenon (see Figure 5). When motivation is weak, performance is poor, and as motivation becomes stronger, performance improves — but only to a point. Performance level eventually

Figure 5
Motivation and Performance: The Inverted U

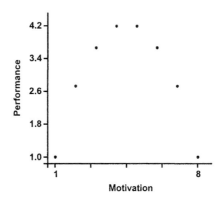

Box 2
Simpson's Paradox - Categorical Data
and Confounding

You are presented with the following categorical data: over the past 5 years, 3,000 out of 10,000 women applicants for graduate work at Ames University were accepted, while 3,500 out of 10,000 male applicants were accepted. Using the Z test for proportions, you determine that the difference in acceptance rates is highly statistically significant. You conclude that there is a prima facie case for gender discrimination in graduate admissions at Ames University.

Further inquiry elicits the following information: There are three graduate schools at Ames: the law school, the medical school and the business school. When broken down by school, the admissions data looks like this: for the medical school, 300 of 3,000 male applicants were accepted (10%), versus 900 of 6,000 female applicants (15%); for the law school, 1,200 out of 3,000 males (40%) were accepted, versus 1,500 out of 3,000 females (50%), for the business school 2,000 males were accepted out of 4,000 male applicants (50%) versus 600 females out of 1,000 (60%).

So, when the data is broken down by school, each of the 3 schools is found to admit a higher percentage of its female applicants than of its male applicants. Do you wish to reconsider your initial assessment of the probability of gender discrimination?

---

drops off, because of factors such as anxiety resulting from excessive motivation. (For example, if your life were at stake, your performance would likely be seriously impaired, even though you'd be very highly motivated to perform well.) The strong, regular relationship between the two variables is unmistakable. The correlation between motivation and performance is, nevertheless, zero.

2. Correlation and prediction. Although correlation doesn't imply causation, it does imply that a value of either variable for a given subject can be used to predict the value of the other variable for that subject. And the higher the absolute value of the correlation coefficient for the two variables, the better the prediction will be. Consider for a moment LSAT scores and first-year law school grades, which we concluded aren't causally related despite being moderately correlated. Is it, then, a mistake to use a student's LSAT score to make a rough prediction of that about a student's first-year grades? No, it isn't. What a positive correlation says about the relationship between variables is that higher values of one variable tend to be paired with higher values of the other variable and lower values with lower values. Thus, for example, predicting that first-year GPA will be higher than average for a student whose LSAT score was higher than average and lower than average for a student whose LSAT score was lower than average would be perfectly justifiable (and even more specific predictions are possible, though we will need the material in the next section to make them.)

A lack of information about causation simply implies that we can't predictably change the value of one of two correlated variables by intervening and manipulating the value of the other one. Imagine, for example, that we could persuade the LSAT scorers to raise a student's score. Could we conclude that the student's first-year GPA would be higher than it would have been had the LSAT score not been bumped upward? Though we might not be tempted to answer this question in the affirmative, we could probably be more easily led to believe, solely on the basis of correlational studies, that drinking wine is good for the heart or that increasing teachers' salaries improves student performance.

D. Simple Linear Regression

Correlational analysis is useful for roughly identifying the strength and direction of a linear relationship between two variables. So, when a loose, qualitative prediction (e.g., that Mary will be taller than average) is good enough, as is sometimes the case, correlational analysis is up to the task. Often, however, a more

> **Box 3**
> **Correlational Analysis:**
> **A Controversial Application**
>
> A recent book by a well-known public health researcher offers the following advice to parents – "It is well known that the earlier a child takes his first drink, the more likely he will be an alcoholic in later life, so do all you can to delay your child's first experience of alcohol." Is this advice justified by the cited results?

specific, quantitative prediction is desirable or necessary. In such cases we would like to identify the specific linear equation that will produce, on average, the best estimates of the value of the variable to be predicted.

Simple linear regression is a technique for deriving and using this optimal linear equation. The variable whose value is to be predicted is called the *response variable,* and the variable from which the prediction is to be made is the *explanatory variable.* Because linear regression depends only on correlational information and correlation is bidirectional (i.e., if A is correlated with B, then B is correlated with A), either of the correlated variables may be designated the response variable.

Here's an example of the use of a simple linear regression equation.

Example 2

Hazel, a 40-year-old mother, is 66 inches tall, and she'd like to know how tall her 6-year-old daughter, Emily, will be at age 20. She knows that the heights of mothers and daughters are correlated and thus that it's possible to predict daughter's height from mother's height,[4] but she doesn't

---

4. Mother's height could just as easily be predicted from daughter's height, in which case mother's height would be the response variable and daughter's height the explanatory variable.

know how to do it. So she turns to us.

We just happen to have a simple regression equation for predicting the height (in inches) of a 20-year-old daughter (let's call this height E) from the height (in inches) of her mother at age 40 years (H)[5]:

$$E = 28 \text{ inches} + (0.6 \times H)$$

We also know that Hazel, at age 40 years, is 66 inches tall, so we plug 66 into the equation:

$$E = 28 + (0.6 \times 66)$$
$$= 28 + 39.6$$
$$= 67.6$$

We can tell Hazel that Emily is predicted to be 67.6 inches tall when she's 20 years old.

As you may have noticed, the equation that we just used has the general form of a linear equation, $y = a + bx$, where x and y represent variables and a and b are constants. And because a linear equation is the formula for a straight line, when pairs of values for the two variables of any given simple regression equation are plotted in a scatterplot, they lie on a perfectly straight line[6] called the *regression line* for that particular regression equation. The value of one of the constants, a, determines where the regression line intersects the y-axis. Hence, a is known as the *y-intercept*. The value of the other constant, b, which is called the *regression coefficient*, defines the angle of the regression line. 'b' is also referred to as the *slope* of the regression line. When b is a positive value, we

---

5. This equation was derived from the heights of 500 pairs of mothers and daughters. The actual derivation was a complicated, messy task — one that's best left to computers.

6. If this concept isn't familiar, take a moment to check it out. Label the y-axis of a graph "daughter's height" and the x-axis "mother's height." Choose three or four values for mother's height, calculate daughter's height for each, and plot the pairs of heights. You can also plot the pair of values from the example ($x = 66.0$, $y = 67.6$). A single straight line can be drawn through all of the plotted points.

can be certain both that the line goes *upward* from left to right and that y (the value predicted for the response variable) *increases* if x increases. When b is negative, on the other hand, the line goes *downward* from left to right and y *decreases* if x increases.

The best linear equation for prediction has a corresponding regression line (and every regression line has a corresponding linear equation). Hence, for any two correlated variables, finding the best linear equation for prediction (i.e., the one that yields the best predictions possible) is equivalent to finding the straight line that comes closest to the points of the scatterplot.[7] The closeness of the regression line to the points on the scatterplot is known as the *fit* of the regression line to the data. The fit is perfect when all the points fall squarely on the line. For fit to be perfect, the correlation must be perfect — that is, the correlation coefficient between the explanatory variable and the response variable must be exactly +1.0 or –1.0. Otherwise, the degree of fit depends on the definition of closeness adopted. We'll illustrate this definitional problem in the following example.

Example 3

We've just been informed that the personnel file on one Starchway employee, employee 21, was inadvertently left out of the batch of files provided to us when we did our initial analysis of salaries at the company. Even though the file still isn't available and we don't know anything particular about the employee, we'd like to estimate the employee's salary.

Our best guess at employee 21's salary is $60,000, the mean of the salary distribution.[8] (In the absence of additional useful information, the best guess at an unknown value from a distribution is, for most purposes, the mean of the distribution.)

---

7. As we'll see in a moment, *best* and *closest* require further elucidation to function as regression criteria.

8. An argument could be made, of course, that a more appropriate estimate would be the mean calculated with Ms. Starchway's salary excluded.

Employee 21's personnel file has been delivered to us. We can't, however, find any record of the employee's current salary, though we can determine that the employee has 9 years of relevant experience. What's our best estimate now?

Knowing that experience and salary are correlated and knowing how much relevant experience employee 21 has, we can apply linear regression analysis to make an estimate of the employee's salary that's likely to be better than our original estimate. We'll treat salary, which we'll designate as S, as the response variable, and relevant experience, E, as the explanatory variable, so,

$$S = a + (b \times E)$$

where we will determine from our data what values for the two constants, a and b, yield the best linear equation for prediction.

The best linear equation for prediction will be the one that describes the line which lies closest to the points in the scatterplot of salary and experience (Figure 1). Figure 6 offers some candidate regression lines. As you can see, it's not obvious which line fits the description "closest to the points," because each line is closer to some points than any of the other lines, but further from others. What we need is a measure of overall closeness, one that in some way takes into account all the distances between the data points and the line. The sum of the distances between each point and the line might seem the obvious candidate, but for technical reasons, the sum of the *squared* distances is preferred.[9] So, from a statistical perspective, the line that's 'closest' to all the points and thus the best choice for the regression line is the one for which the sum of the squared distances between the data points and the line is the smallest possible. This line is called the *least squares regression line*, and the equation for this line is the *ordinary least squares* (OLS) estimator.

---

9. Specifically, we use the vertical distance between each point and the line.

Example 3 *(continued)*

        The OLS estimator for our data on Starchway salary and experience turns out to be

$$S = 35{,}278.89 + 4{,}754.06(E)$$

where S is salary (in dollars) and E is relevant experience (in years). The constant b (4,754.06) in the OLS estimator of the Starchway data can be interpreted as a measure of how much 1 year of relevant experience is worth, on average, in terms of salary. In other words, every year of relevant experience that a Starchway employee has is worth an average

Figure 6
Candidate Regression Lines

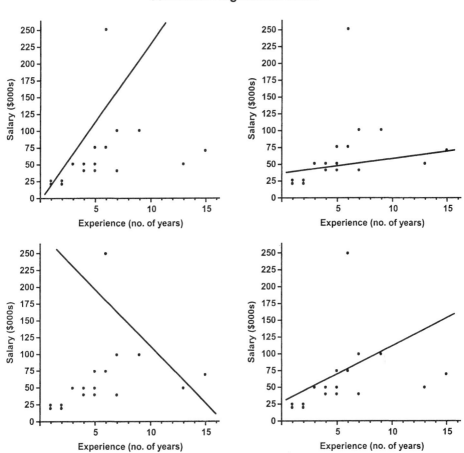

of $4,754.06 in salary. The constant a (35,278.89) can be interpreted as the starting salary of a worker with no experience. The line itself can be seen on the scatterplot in Figure 7. Using this equation, our best estimate of employee 21's salary from linear regression analysis is

$$S = 35,278.89 + (4,754.06 \times E)$$
$$= 35,278.89 + (4,754.06 \times 9)$$
$$= 78,065.43$$

How good is our new prediction likely to be? It depends on how strongly the explanatory variable (experience) is correlated with the response variable (salary). The correlation coefficient of 0.3289 for experience and salary indicates that the correlation between the two variables is weakly positive. We can't, then, expect our prediction to be very accurate. To get a sense of the overall accuracy of our OLS estimator, we can compare the estimated salaries calculated from the equation for employees 1–20 with the actual salaries, which we know.

Let's look at Table 3, where the actual salary of each employee is listed along with the corresponding estimate calculated from the regression equation and the residual for each of the two esti-

Figure 7
Starchway Salaries: The Best-Fitting Line

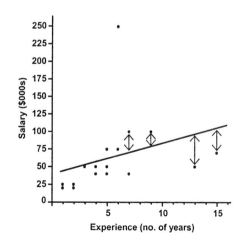

mates of salary, the regression-generated estimate and the mean of all employee salaries. (A residual is simply the difference between a true value and an estimated value.) It's immediately apparent from the residuals that the regression estimates certainly aren't perfect, though they do seem, on average, to be better estimates than the mean is.

A statistic, R^2, is frequently used to express the accuracy of the estimates provided by a regression equation. All the information necessary to calculate R^2 for our regression equation is in Table 3.

Table 3
Starchway Salaries: The Residuals

Employee	Actual salary ($)	Regression derived estimate ($)	Regression residual ($)	Residual using mean ($60,000) as estimate ($)
1	25,000	44,787.01	−19,787.01	−35,000
2	50,000	54,295.13	−4,295.13	−10,000
3	40,000	54,295.13	−14,295.13	−20,000
4	75,000	59,049.19	15,950.81	15,000
5	40,000	68,557.31	−28,557.31	20,000
6	50,000	97,081.67	−47,081.67	10,000
7	20,000	40,032.95	−20,032.95	40,000
8	50,000	73,311.37	−23,311.37	10,000
9	50,000	73,311.37	−23.311.37	10,000
10	70,000	106,589.79	36,589.79	10,000
11	25,000	40,032.95	−15,032.95	35,000
12	20,000	44,787.01	−24,787.01	40,000
13	250,000	63,803.25	186,196.75	190,000
14	100,000	78,065.43	21,934.57	40,000
15	75,000	63,803.25	11,196.75	15,000
16	50,000	59,049.19	−9,049.19	10,000
17	20,000	40,032.95	−20,032.95	40,000
18	50,000	49,541.07	458.93	10,000
19	100,000	68,557.31	31,442.69	40,000
20	40,000	59,049.19	−19,049.19	20,000

How to . . .

. . . calculate R^2

1. Using the mean of each response variable as an estimate of its residual, add the squared residuals for all variables to find the total sum of squares (TSS):

$$TSS = residual_{(mean)_1}{}^2 + residual_{(mean)_2}{}^2 + \ldots$$
$$+ \, residual_{(mean)_n}{}^2$$

2. Then, using the estimated residual derived for each variable from the regression equation, add the squared residuals for all variables to get the sum of squared residuals (SSR):

$$SSR = residual_{(regression)_1}{}^2 + residual_{(regression)_2}{}^2 + \ldots$$
$$+ \, residual_{(regression)_n}{}^2$$

3. Subtract the sum of the squared residuals from the total sum of squares to find the reduction in the total that's achieved by estimating with the regression equation rather than with the mean, and divide the difference by the total sum of squares to get the proportionate reduction, which is R^2:

$$R^2 = \frac{TSS - SSR}{TSS}$$

4. Optionally, convert the calculated R^2 to a percent. When expressed as a percent, R^2 is often referred to as the *percentage of variance explained.* (Why is this term appropriate? Think about how the total sum of squares is related to variance.)

$$R^2(\%) = \frac{TSS - SSR}{TSS} \times 100$$

An R^2 of 0 indicates that the error in the estimate calculated from the regression equation is no less than that associated with the mean as estimate. In other words, the explanatory variable is of no use at all in predicting the response variable. An R^2 of 1.0, on the other hand, indicates that there is no error in the regression-

generated estimates and thus that the explanatory variable predicts the response variable perfectly.

So what is R-squared for our Starchway regression?

Example 4

  1. Calculate the TSS:

  Square the residuals resulting from using the mean as
  estimator and add them together TSS = 48,900,000,000.

  2. Then calculate the SSR:

  Square the residuals resulting from using the regression
  equation as estimator and add them together SSR =
  43,609,000,000.

  3. Subtract the SSR from the TSS:

  48,900,000,000 − 43,609,000,000 = 5,291,000,000. This
  is the reduction in the squared errors resulting from using
  the regression equation.

  4. Calculate R^2

  $$\frac{5,291,000,000}{48,900,000,000} = .1082$$

  5. Convert R^2 to a percent reduction in squared error
  .1082 × 100 = 10.82%

We now know that the equation will reduce the average
squared error about 11%. Put another way, the equation explains
about 11% of the variation in employees' salaries.[10] Remember,
though, that this R-squared was calculated from a given data set
and therefore, claiming that it applies to predictions made about
individuals outside the given data set is a matter of inference,
which involves problems of randomness, sample size, and so forth.

---

10. *Explains* is commonly used in this context even though use of the word
generally isn't justified. It should be clear from what you know about how
R^2 is calculated that the claim of explanation goes beyond the available evidence. Think back to the temperature example that we considered earlier in
the chapter. The R^2 for a regression equation that predicts Fahrenheit temperatures from Celsius temperatures would be 1.0 — that is, the equation
would be perfect in its predictions. But would you say that Celsius temperature perfectly *explains* Fahrenheit temperature?

You may have noticed that the R^2 for our Starchway regression is exactly equal to the square of the correlation coefficient, r, for salary and experience: $R^2 = 0.1082$ and $r^2 = 0.3289^2 = 0.1082$. That the two are identical is no accident. Rather, it's the result of a general phenomenon that relates correlation and simple regression. (Are you surprised that the statistic is dubbed R-squared?) While R^2 is calculated in the same way for multiple regression equations, in the multiple regression context it no longer bears such a straightforward relationship to the correlation coefficient.

E. Residuals

Residuals are of interest for much more than their role in calculating R^2. Let's return to the Starchway residuals for the regression estimates. A simple way to visually organize them is to plot them as in Figure 8. A plot of this sort is particularly useful for identifying individuals in the data set for whom the explanatory variable is especially poor at predicting the actual response variable. Such individuals are routinely accorded special attention, because unusual residuals suggest that the these individuals may be subject to some factor that doesn't generally affect the others in the data set. A residual that's far out of line with the majority poses a problem analogous to the one posed by outliers in one-variable distributions. As with outliers, such residuals may arise from legitimate values of the variable in question. But because of their disproportionate effect on the results of a variety of statistical analyses of the data, the data values that produced them are scrutinized carefully and may be excluded from certain statistical calculations. Because the OLS estimator is designed to minimize *squared* errors, the problem of unusual values can be particularly acute in the regression context. A list of individuals that generate unusual residuals, or *influential observations,* as they're often referred to, usually appears on the regression printout.

From the plot of the Starchway residuals, the residual associated with the salary for employee 13, Mary Starchway, appears

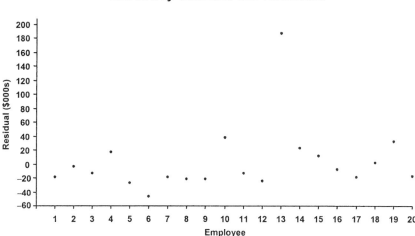

Figure 8
Starchway Salaries: The Residuals

to be just as influential as the salary itself was as an outlier. Do all outliers in one-variable data sets appear as influential observations in regression analyses? (Do all influential observations in regression analyses appear as outliers in one-variable data sets?)

Plots such as Figure 8 for the Starchway data may also can reveal patterns in residuals that suggest that some important variable other than the two in the regression equation is at play. Plotting the residuals against the times at which the matching observations were made, for example, might yield a pattern like the one in Figure 9. In such a case, it appears that the regression equation from which the residuals were derived predicted past values very well but appears to be doing much worse recently. Is some new factor affecting the relationship between the response variable and the predictor variable?

F. Limitations of Linear Regression

Linear regression analysis has important limitations. For example, although the relationship between two variables may take any of a number of forms, a linear equation is an effective predictor only if the relationship is approximately linear (i.e., only if the scatterplot has a roughly linear appearance). The larger the abso-

Figure 9
Hypothetical Stock Index : Regression Residuals

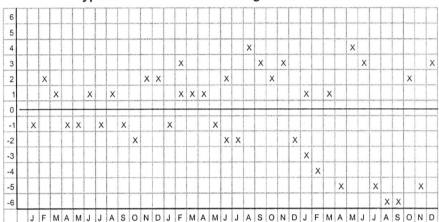

lute value of the correlation coefficient of the two variables, the better the linear regression equation is in its predictions.

A second limitation is that a linear regression equation predicts the same value for the response variable for all individuals with a given value on the explanatory variable. For example, using the regression equation on page 72, a height of 67.6 inches is predicted at age 20 for every daughter whose mother at age 40 was 66.0 inches tall. It takes just a moment, though, to realize that this outcome is extremely unlikely. Rather, the daughters of mothers who were 66.0 inches when they were 40 years old constitute a subpopulation of all daughters. And because this subpopulation has a height distribution of its own, no single predicted value can possibly be correct for all its members. In fact, for any given value of an explanatory variable, variability in the value of the response variable is the norm rather than the exception. For this reason, error is virtually unavoidable in regression analysis.

2. Multiple Regression

Multiple regression may be viewed as an extension of simple regression to data sets with more than two variables. To accommodate the additional variables, the regression equation is expanded to include more than one explanatory variable $(x_1, x_2, \ldots, x_n)$, each paired with its own regression coefficient $(b_1, b_2, \ldots, b_n)$. Thus, the general form of a multiple regression equation is $y = a + x_1 b_1 + x_2 b_2 + \ldots + x_n b_n$. For example, a multiple regression equation for predicting life expectancy (the response variable) for 25-year-old males on the basis of four explanatory variables — systolic blood pressure, cigarette smoking, weight, and formal education — might be

$$L = 51 - (0.03 \times P) - (0.2 \times C) - (0.1 \times W) + (0.3 \times S)$$

where L represents life expectancy in number of years, P represents systolic blood pressure in millimeters of mercury (mm Hg), C represents cigarette smoking in number of packs per week, W represents weight in percent above ideal, and S represents formal schooling in number of years. Just as with simple regression, a predicted score for an individual is calculated by multiplying the individual's score on each explanatory variable by its regression coefficient and then adding all the products plus the value of the y intercept (the value of the constant a) together. (What's the predicted life expectancy of a 25-year-old male who has a systolic blood pressure of 90 mm Hg, weighs 10% more than the ideal, smokes 4 packs of cigarettes a week, and has completed 19 years of school? Can you explain the negative coefficient for the cigarette-smoking variable?)

As with simple regression, the best equation for a multiple regression analysis is the one whose calculated intercept and coefficients (a and $b_1, b_2, \ldots, b_n$, respectively) minimize the sum of the squared errors of prediction. This equation, the OLS multiple regression equation, can be evaluated in much the same way as the simple linear regression equation was: by comparing, for each individual in the data set, its prediction of the response variable, y, with the alternative prediction of the response variable, its mean. If we knew nothing about a particular 25-year-old male, we would predict an average life expectancy for him, but if we knew something about his blood pressure, our prediction could be better. And if we also knew whether or how much he smokes, it would be better still. In fact, the more *relevant* information we have, the better our prediction would be, because multiple regression uses the additional information to improve predictive accuracy.

Multiple regression is eminently suited to the task of analyzing complex phenomena that result from the interplay of many variables. Crime rates, law school grades, employee salaries, business profits, inflation, and election outcomes are just a few examples. For such phenomena to be fully understood, not only must the contributory factors be identified, but the relative contribution of each must be quantified. For example, we might want to know what impact a change in the unemployment rate would have on the violent crime rate. Using a *simple* regression approach, we would check to see that unemployment and crime rate are correlated, and then produce a simple linear regression equation relating the two. Such an approach, while better than nothing, is subject to the common response problem (perhaps unemployment doesn't cause crime, but some third variable, e.g. lack of education, causes both to move together) and the problem of confounding variables (for example, both unemployment and crime have seasonal components).

Remember, as we emphasized above, correlation doesn't imply causation. To fully understand the relationship between unemployment and crime we have to account for the impacts on both of other related variables like education and season, and this is not possible within the restricted domain of simple regression. Multiple regression, on the other hand, allows us to take account of all additional relevant factors for which we have data. We develop a multiple regression equation that includes all relevant explanatory variables (or least as many as practicable) and then focus on the coefficient of the variable of interest — here, unemployment rate. This coefficient, unlike the simple regression coefficient, reflects the magnitude of the relationship between unemployment rate and crime when the influence of the other predictor variables is accounted for.

Consider the following regression equation (which, admittedly, falls far short of the ideal of including all relevant variables), where C represents the crime rate (in number of crimes per 100,000 population), T represents the average monthly temperature (in degrees Fahrenheit), D represents the high school dropout rate (in percent), and U represents the unemployment rate (in percent):

$$C = 200 + 1.2T + 2D + 40U$$

The analyst would conclude that, when temperature and dropout rate are controlled for (i.e. accounted for), each 1.0 percentage point increase in the unemployment rate is associated with, on average, an additional 40 violent crimes per 100,000 population.

Multiple regression is also used for prediction of a response variable, just as with simple linear regression. The difference is that, with multiple regression, enormous amounts of additional information can be brought to bear. Equations created to predict the future course of the U.S. economy contain literally hundreds of explanatory variables.

A. Multiple Regression and Discrimination Litigation

Multiple regression analysis is often used in discrimination litigation to isolate the impact of a single explanatory variable on a response variable, such as the decision to hire. In litigation of a claim of gender discrimination in wages, for example, a plaintiff could make a prima facie case by pointing out that the average salary for women at the defendant company is less than the average salary for men. The defense might argue that the discrepancy has arisen not because of discrimination, but simply because the women on the company's payroll happen to have, on average, less education and experience than the men do and the defendant, perfectly legitimately, rewards its employees who have more education and experience by paying them higher salaries. In other words, the average salary is higher for the men because they are, as a group, the more educated and more experienced employees. The plaintiff would love to be able to rebut this argument with data on women employees whose experience and education are comparable to men's but whose wages are lower. Unfortunately, in a particular workforce, there may be few women for whom such a direct comparison is possible. Multiple regression analysis, via a mathematically complex averaging process, is able to generate precisely the sort of comparison that the plaintiff has in mind.

Using data on the relevant variables from the defendant's employment records, the plaintiff would construct a multiple regression equation with wage as the response variable. Letting W stand for wage in dollars, S for number of years of schooling (or education), E for number of years of experience, and G for gender,[11] suppose that the multiple regression equation that the plaintiff ended up with turned out to be

$$W = 23{,}000 + (2{,}000 \times S) + (3{,}100 \times E) - (7{,}000 \times G)$$

This regression equation predicts, for example, that the average

---

11. Gender is a categorical variable, and for this reason, it receives special treatment (as does any categorical variable included as an explanatory variable in a regression equation). Because there are two possible "values" of gender, female and male, one (female) was assigned a numerical value of 1 and the other (male) a numerical value of 0. A categorical variable whose possible values are assigned numerical values of 0 and 1 for the purpose of inclusion in multiple regression equations is known as a *dummy variable*. It doesn't matter which numerical value the 0 or the 1 is applied to which gender; the assignment is arbitrary. In the equation here, 1 could just as well have been assigned to male and 0 to female. Had this been the case, the gender coefficient would have turned out to be +7,000 instead of -7,000.

salary for female employees with 16 years of education and 6 years of experience would be $66,600:

$$23,000 + (2,000 \times 16) + (3,100 \times 6) - (7,000 \times 1) = \$66,600$$

The prediction for male employees with the same amount of education and experience, on the other hand, would be $73,600:

$$23,000 + (2,000 \times 16) + (3,100 \times 6) + (7,000 \times 0) = \$73,600$$

It's easy to see that for any combination of education and experience, the average female employee would be paid $7,000 less than the average male with exactly the same combination of education and experience, or, to put it into statistical language, after controlling for education and experience, women employees are paid $7,000 less than men. And this is exactly the type of demonstration that the plaintiff was hoping to present.

Let's look at an example of this sort of application of multiple regression analysis from an actual case.

Example 5

Bazemore et al. v. Friday et al., 478 U.S. 385 (1986)

This case centered around an allegation of racial discrimination in salary at the North Carolina Agricultural Extension Service. The average annual salary of black employees was substantially below that of whites. However, blacks tended to have less education and job experience. Data on salary, race, and legitimate factors that affect wages (education and job experience among others) were analyzed by multiple regression to determine whether the racial disparity in salary remained when the other factors were controlled for. Table 4 summarizes the explanatory variables that were included in the equation to predict annual salary, the scoring system for these variables, and the regression results. When all other factors were controlled for, being white added, on average, about $395 to salary.

Standard error is a version of the standard deviation for regression coefficients. Because each regression coefficient (b_x) is derived from a sample, it's an estimate of the corresponding parameter

Table 4
Bazemore et al. v. Friday et al.: Explanatory Variables
and Scoring System Used in Multiple Regression Analysis

Explanatory variables and scoring system

Variable	Score
Education	
master's degree (MS)	1 if person has master's degree; 0 otherwise
Employment	
tenure (TENURE)	number of years with the Service as of 1975
Position	
chairman (CHM)	1 if chairman; 0 otherwise
agent (AGENT)	1 if agent; 0 otherwise
associate (ASSOC)	1 if associate agent; 0 otherwise
Race (WHITE)	1 if white; 0 otherwise

Results

Response variable: annual salary

Explanatory variable	Coefficient	Standard error
MS	898.55	140.36
TENURE	59.06	8.47
CHM	5,221.19	232.28
AGENT	2,404.44	170.58
ASSOC	918.82	174.42
WHITE	394.80	137.67
CONSTANT	9,291.51	(none given)

Adjusted R-squared: 0.76

(the regression coefficient for the entire population, B_x). The larger the sample, the smaller the standard error of the regression coefficient tends to be and the smaller the difference between the coefficient for the sample and the coefficient for the population is likely to be.

There's always a possibility that what regression analysis identifies as an association between a response variable and an explanatory variable is only an apparent association, not a genuine association, the result of unknowingly working with a sample that's unusual in some way and thus not truly representative of the population. For this reason, standard practice is to test each regression coefficient to determine whether there's good reason to think that the corresponding coefficient for the population isn't 0. A null hypothesis is formulated for each regression coefficient — that the regression coefficient is 0 (i.e., $b_x = 0$) — and the hypothesis is tested. In this setting, the t test is the appropriate hypothesis test to use.

How to . . .

. . . perform a t test

1. Divide the regression coefficient for the sample, b_x, by its standard error to calculate its t score (the distance, measured in standard errors, that the coefficient is from 0).[12]

$$t = \frac{b_x}{\text{standard error for } b_x}$$

2. Subtract the number of regression coefficients (which we'll abbreviate as c for the sake of simplicity), including the constant, in the equation being tested from n, the number of individuals in the sample from which the regression equation was derived to find the number of degrees of freedom (df)[13]:

$$df = n - c$$

3. Look in the t table (see page 106) to find the t score that corresponds to the number of degrees of freedom at the 0.05 significance level (or whatever significance level has been set as the standard to be met). To do this, look in the column labeled df for the appropriate number. Look across that row until you reach the column labeled 0.05. The number in this cell is the t score for the number of degrees of freedom at the 0.05 significance level.

---

12. Calculating a t score no doubt reminds you of calculating a z score. The processes are quite similar, but the t table is a bit more complicated to use than the z table is.

13. Degrees of freedom is a technical concept the explanation of which is beyond the scope of this handbook. You don't, however, have to understand it to be able to use the t table.

4. If the calculated t score for the regression coefficient is greater than the t score in the table, you can reject the null hypothesis (i.e., $b_x = 0$) and conclude that the regression coefficient for x is statistically significant at the 0.05 level.

Let's test the null hypothesis for one of the regression coefficients — tenure — from the *Bazemore* case.

Example 6

1. We divide the regression coefficient for tenure by the corresponding standard error to get the coefficient's t score:

$$t = \frac{59.06}{8.47}$$
$$= 6.97$$

2. Then, to determine the number of degrees of freedom, we subtract the number of regression coefficients (which is 7, including the constant) from the sample size (which, though not specified earlier, is 568):

$$df = 568 - 7$$
$$= 561$$

3. Our next step is to find the t score that corresponds to 561 degrees of freedom at the 0.05 significance level. But when we look down the column labeled df in the t table, we see that no numbers between 120 and infinity are listed. Let's be conservative and thus opt to use the t score for 120 degrees of freedom. Locating the cell where the row for 120 degrees of freedom intersects with the column for the 0.05 significance level, we find that the t score is 1.980.

4. Because the t score that we calculated (6.97) is greater than the t score corresponding to 120 degrees of freedom at the 0.05 significance level (1.980), we can reject the null hypothesis (i.e., $b_{tenure} = 0$) and conclude that the regression coefficient for tenure is statistically significant at the 0.05 level.[14]

---

14. In fact, all of the regression coefficients in the Bazemore equation are significant at the 0.05 level. You might want to verify this claim by testing the null hypothesis for each of the other regression coefficients.

What if a regression coefficient fails to pass the t test at the desired level of significance? In such an event, we can't conclude that the explanatory variable associated with it has a statistically significant effect on the response variable when all the other explanatory variables in the equation are controlled for. Failure to reach the specified level of significance is most troubling when the variable is the one of particular interest. For example, finding that the coefficient for race in the *Bazemore* case didn't meet the criterion for statistical significance would be a serious blow to the plaintiff's case.[15] If the coefficient that fails the t test is for an explanatory variable other than the one that's the focus of the inquiry, calculating a new regression equation from which the questioned variable is omitted and noting the impact that the omission has on R-squared would be appropriate. If the change in R-squared is small, the revised equation may well be preferable. The decision is ultimately a judgment call by the analyst, taking into consideration nonstatistical matters, such as the nature of the underlying scientific theory.

B. Things That Can Go Wrong

In our experience, badly conducted regression analysis is the norm rather than the exception in social science and legal writing. Because of the substantial leeway accorded the analyst in choosing explanatory variables and finding or generating data, it is possible for sophisticated analysts to represent a much more favorable view of their preferred theories than would be justified by a more balanced treatment of the evidence. Less sophisticated researchers too often miss the mark, in their case, because of failure to appreciate the considerable subtleties and complexities of regression analysis. In the following sections we will present the deviations from sound practice that you will most frequently encounter along with some idea of the distortions that may result

---

15. There would, however, be room for argument over the appropriateness of a 0.05 significance level in a civil case, where the overall evidentiary standard is preponderance of the evidence.

and what to do about them.

1. Omission of important explanatory variables. Whether important explanatory variables have been omitted from a regression equation is an issue that is at the heart of many discrimination cases. For example, in *EEOC v. Sears* (839 F.2d 302, 1988), Sears, the defendant in a sex discrimination suit, claimed that women were less likely to be in high-paying jobs in commission sales at Sears because, as a group, they lacked interest in work of this type, not because Sears discriminated against women in hiring. According to the defense's theory, a woman who expressed an interest in commission sales would have about the same chance as a man of getting such a position, but this would only be revealed in the regression analysis if interest were included as an explanatory variable. If interest is correlated with being female and if interest is an important determinant of employment in commission sales, then excluding interest from the regression equation would lead to an incorrect (i.e. inflated) estimate of the effect that being female has on the chance of getting a job in commission sales.

It's important to note here that the problem arises not simply because a variable with the potential to affect hiring is left out of the equation. Many factors affect hiring decisions, ones that are measurable as well as ones that aren't. For the most part, they can be ignored as long as they aren't correlated with the variables that <u>are</u> included. The regression may have less explanatory power overall (i.e., a smaller R^2), but the interpretation of the significance and magnitude of the coefficients of the included variables won't be tainted. When the omitted variable is, however, significantly correlated with one or more included variables, then the regression coefficients of the correlated variables will be biassed.

As an example of the consequences of omitting an important variable that's correlated with an included variable, consider this equation for hourly wage, which includes as explanatory variables education (E), age (A), race (R; 1 if the individual is white, 0 otherwise), and marital status (M; 1 if the individual is married, 0 if not):

$$W = -12 + (1.2 \times E) + (0.2 \times A) + (1.5 \times R) + (1.7 \times M)$$

According to these estimates, married men earn, on average, $1.70 an hour more than unmarried men with the same characteristics. However, if we omit age from the equation but otherwise use the same data, the equation becomes

$$W = -6 + (1.2 \times E) + (1.3 \times R) + (3.2 \times M)$$

Now the implication is that married men are paid, not $1.70 an hour more, but $3.20 an hour more than their unmarried counterparts. When age is omitted from the equation, its effect is picked up by the coefficients of the other variables in the model.

Notice that the coefficient for education didn't change and the one for race changed only slightly. The reason for this is that the correlation between education and age is weak (once people complete their education), as is the correlation between race and age. However, the correlation between marital status and age is fairly strong: older men are more likely than younger men to be married. The effect of age on earnings is rolled into the marriage coefficient, and the result is an artificially inflated estimate of the influence of marriage on wage.

2. Inclusion of irrelevant variables. Obviously, when the goal is to explain the response variable, the ideal is for all of the variables involved in producing the observed variation in the response variable (and only these variables) to be included in the regression model. Typically, this standard is quite difficult to achieve. Variables are included and excluded as the analysis proceeds, and different models are tested against the data. Candidates for inclusion as explanatory variables come from two sources: preexisting theories about the phenomenon being investigated and data sets that allow for the statistical testing of possible associations. Such possibly relevant variables are included in trial regressions. Depending on the sizes of the resulting regression coefficients, the magnitude of the R-squared, and the levels of significance revealed by the t tests, they may be included in, or excluded from, the final regression model.

There is a problem is inherent in this approach. If too many variables are tested for possible relevance, a small percentage of them will, simply because of sampling error appear, to be significant when in fact they aren't. If these variables are erroneously included in the final regression model, not only will spurious relationships be presented as real, but the coefficients calculated for the variables that *are* relevant will be, on average, worse estimates of the corresponding population coefficients.

3. Multicollinearity. Most economic variables are correlated with one another to some extent. For instance, number of years of work experience and age are highly correlated for college-educated men. If both age and experience are included in a wage equation, isolating the effect of age on wage from the effect of work experience on wage may be difficult, and statistically, neither variable may appear to be a significant determinant of wage. This type of problem is the result of multicollinearity. Although the temptation may be to drop one of the variables creating the problem, doing so may introduce bias if both variables are important determinants of wage.

Multicollinearity can be used to make effects that would otherwise be statistically significant disappear. For example, we can define makeup use as a variable. Since makeup use and being female are highly correlated, including both variables in a wage regression is likely to yield an insignificant effect of being female on wage. Although this example may seem silly and extreme, an econometrician can, quite easily and subtly, add in variables that will make the variable of concern appear insignificant. In contrast, including fewer variables will increase the apparent importance of the variables that are retained.

Usually, the solution to multicollinearity is to obtain better, more refined data — not to throw out important variables.

4. Two-way causation. Do police have a damping effect on the violent crime rate? Most people would say that the answer is obviously yes. It might seem obvious then that, in a multiple regression equation with police (number per 1,000 residents) as an explanatory variable and violent crime rate (e.g., number of violent crimes per 1,000 residents) as the response variable, the regression coefficient for police should be negative, an indication that violent crime rate decreases as police presence increases. Surprisingly, however, the coefficient is likely to be near 0 or even positive: While it is true that sending more police to a particular area will tend to reduce the crime rate in that area, it is also true that more police will be sent to areas that have higher crime rates. Changing the concentration of police changes the crime rate (more police, fewer crimes) but changing the crime rate changes the concentration of police (as the crime rate drops in a particular area, police are shifted away from that area). This is an example of the two-way causation problem, which arises when an explanatory variable causes changes in a response variable, while at the same time changes in the response variable cause changes in the explanatory variable. In such a situation, the regression coefficient for the explanatory variable in question is biased. Solving a two-way causation problem is, generally, not easy, and the methods are outside the scope of the text.[16] Another instance of the simultaneity problem occurs in the following situation: a researcher hypothesizes that the more money spent per pupil on primary and high school education in a school district, the better the resulting education. Yet, when the researcher produces a regression equation with achievement test scores as the response variable and per pupil spending as an explanatory variable, the regression coefficient on per pupil spending is negative, indicating that the less money spent per pupil, the better on average the achieve-

---

16. Chapters 10 & 11 of the Stock and Watson text cited on the following page present the two most common approaches to the problem of two-way causation.

ment test scores. Can you use the two way causation idea to explain this result?

3. Suggestions for Further Reading

Many complexities of multivariate statistics were glossed over or, indeed, entirely omitted from this chapter. If you'd like to delve deeper into the subject — whether out of pure intellectual curiosity or out of a practical need to know more — the following works will be helpful.

Laurence G. Grimm and Paul R. Yarnold, eds., *Reading and Understanding Multivariate Statistics* (Washington, D.C.: American Psychological Association, 1995). Presents chapter length treatments of a variety of approaches to multivariate data that may be used as substitutes for or supplements to standard OLS regression, written for the beginning social science graduate student with very little background in math.

Laurence G. Grimm and Paul R. Yarnold, eds., *Reading and Understanding More Multivariate Statistics* (Washington, D.C.: American Psychological Association, 2000).

Peter Kennedy, *A Guide to Econometrics*, 5th Ed. (Cambridge, MA: MIT Press, 2003).

James H. Stock and Mark W. Watson, *Introduction to Econometrics* (Boston: Addison-Wesley, 2003). Slightly less sophisticated than Wooldrige, but with a concluding section of 70 pages presenting the theoretical foundation of econometrics at a graduate level. Also contains a number of thoughtful problems together with solutions, to aid self-study.

Jeffrey M. Wooldrige, *Introductory Econometrics: A Modern Approach* (Mason, Ohio: South-Western Thomson Learning, 2003). A self contained presentation at the undergraduate level, assuming only a basic knowledge of algebra.

The 68%-95%-99.7% Rule: In every normal distribution, about 68% of the values are within 1 standard deviation of the mean, about 95% of the values are within 2 standard deviations, and about 99.7 percent are within 3 standard deviations.

Acquiescence Bias: Bias induced by survey respondents' desire to give the answers the survey designer seems to want.

Chebychev's Rule: For any data set, at least 75% of the data points lie within 2 standard deviations of the mean and at least 89% lie within 3 standard deviations of the mean.

Central Limit Theorem: The theorem postulates that the distribution of the means of random samples of size n from a given population approximates a normal distribution, that it has the same mean as the population from which the samples were drawn and that it has a standard deviation which equals the population standard deviation divided by $\sqrt{n}$.

Common Response Problem: A problem which arises when correlational data are used in an effort to determine causal relationships. If A and B have a strong correlation, is it the result of a direct causal connection between them, or because both respond similarly to changes in a third, unaccounted for, variable?

Confidence Interval: A range of values constructed from sample data in such a way as to have a specific probability of including a true population parameter of interest, as in a 95% confidence interval for the mean.

Confounding: There is said to be confounding when a causal inference based on correlational data is determined to be ill-founded because of the operation of a variable or variables which are not in the original data set.

Confounders: Also called lurking variables, confounders are the unaccounted for variables that produce confounding.

Correlation: Two variables are correlated when the value of either variable can be used to predict the value of other variable for a given subject. Two variables are positively correlated if above average values of one tend to accompany above average values of the other, and vice versa. Two variables are negatively correlated if above average values of one tend to accompany below average values of the other, and vice versa.

Pearson Correlation Coefficient: A number between -1.0 and +1.0 that describes the strength and direction of the linear relationship between two variables. A PCC of -1.0 indicates a perfect negative relationship, +1.0, a perfect positive relationship.

Curve: The graphic representation of a distribution.

Normal Curve: The graphic representation of a normal distribution; it is unimodal and can be divided into two mirror-image halves by an appropriately placed line and thus is symmetric.

Unimodal Curve: A curve characterized by a single mound.

Bimodal Curve: A curve characterized by two mounds.

Data: Bits of information presented in terms of individuals (the units the data are about) and variables (the properties under examination).

Survey Data: Data derived by direct questioning of a sample of individuals chosen from the population being studied.

Data Set: A collection of values of one or more variables for more than one individual.

>**Bivariate Data Set:** A data set consisting of paired values, one score on each of two variables for every individual in the data set.

>**Census:** A data set containing scores on one or more variables for all of the individuals – the entire population – of interest.

>**Multivariate Data Set:** A collection of values that combine two or more one-variable data sets for the same individuals.

>**One-Variable (Univariate) Data Set:** A collection of values of a given variable for more than one individual.

Distribution: The way the values of a variable in a sample or population are related to one another, as is revealed by a histogram or a dot plot.

>**Normal Distribution:** A distribution that has the shape of a normal curve.

>**Rectangular Distribution:** A distribution that has the shape of a rectangle.

>**Sampling Distribution:** The distribution of sample means of a given size, n, drawn from a given population.

>**Skewed Distribution:** A non-symmetric distribution.

Estimator: Any determinate method for producing an estimate from sample data.

Estimation: The use of sample data to make an educated guess about a parameter value, usually the mean, of the population from which a sample was drawn.

Interval estimate: An estimate that specifies both a range of values and the probability that the true value of the parameter is somewhere within this range.

Point estimate: A single value guess at the value of a parameter.

Gaps: Regions in a frequency distribution where there are no or few scores.

Histogram: A kind of bar graph used to pictorially represent a one-variable quantitative data set.

Hypothesis: In statistical hypothesis testing, a claim that a population parameter has some particular value.

> **Null Hypothesis:** The hypothesis that there is no difference between a given population mean and the mean of a random sample taken from a different, but related population.

Individuals: Individuals are the units that data are about. Any object of study can be an individual – a person (e.g. a 24 year old man), a state (e.g. Georgia), an act (e.g. buying a car), a law (e.g. an anti-discrimination statute), etc.

Influential observations: Unusual data points which have a large influence on estimates of regression coefficients.

(Simple) Linear regression: A technique for deriving and using the linear equation that will produce, on average, the best estimates of the variable to be predicted.

Linear relationship: When two variables are linearly related, the value of one can be used to estimate the value of the other via an equation of the form $x = a + by$, where x and y are the variables and a and b are constants.

Measures of Central Tendency

Median: The middle value in a distribution (or, if the distribution contains an even number of values, the average of the middle two values).

Mean: The arithmetic average of the values in a distribution.

Mode: The most frequently occurring value in a distribution.

Measures of Variability or Dispersion

Range: The difference between the lowest and the highest values in the data set.

Standard Deviation: The square root of the variance.

Variance: The mean of the squared deviations of the values in the data set.

Multicollinearity: A problem which arises in multiple regression analysis when an explanatory variable is very closely correlated with other explanatory variables in the same equation. The estimates of the regression coefficients of the correlated variables will be unreliable.

Motivational Bias: A type of bias in survey data resulting from respondents answering survey questions untruthfully in an effort to promote various respondent goals inconsistent with those of the surveyor.

Operationalization: Development of practical measurement techniques or standards that allow for the translation into variables of the properties being studied.

Ordinary Least Squares (OLS) Estimator: The most often used method for producing estimates of regression coefficients.

Outliers: Values that are much lower or higher than the other values in a data set.

Parameters: The numerical descriptors of a population.

Population: The entire set of individuals to be studied.

R^2: A statistic used to express the accuracy of the estimates provided by a regression equation.

Representativeness (of a sample): For any variable, the representativeness of the sample is the degree to which the sample distribution resembles the population from which the sample is taken.

Residual: The difference between a true value and an estimated value.

Sample: A group of individuals selected from the population under study.

> **Convenience Sample:** A sample that comprises individuals who have been chosen because they were relatively accessible.
>
> **Simple Random Sample:** A sample selected in such a way that it is no more and no less likely to be selected than is any other possible sample of the same size. (Note that this is not the same thing as a sample in which each individual has the same chance of being selected.)

Scatterplot: A type of graph on which bivariate data sets are pictorially presented by plotting each individual's scores on both variables as a single point in a two dimensional Cartesian space.

Standard Error: The standard deviation of the sampling distribution of a statistic.

Statistics: The science of collecting, organizing, and interpreting numerical facts.

> **Descriptive Statistics:** The science of describing and organizing sets of data.
>
> **Inferential Statistics:** The science of using data to make predictions about future events or patterns of events (i.e. estimation) and of using data to help confirm or disconfirm hypotheses about the way the world works (i.e. hypothesis testing).
>
> **(As opposed to Parameters):** Numerical descriptors of samples used to estimate parameters.

Statistically Significant Difference: A difference between a given population mean and the mean of a random sample large enough to justify the claim that the sample was taken from a population with a mean different from the mean of the given population.

Type I Error: The rejection of the null hypothesis when it is in fact true.

Type II Error: Failure to reject the null hypothesis when it is in fact false.

Validity: The extent to which a measuring instrument measures what it's intended to measure.

> **Face Validity:** A survey is said to be face valid when it consists of questions that request directly and obviously the information desired by the surveyor.

Variable: A variable can be any property of individuals under study (e.g. height, wealth, aversion to risk, etc), as long as the individuals differ in some way with respect to the property and the differences can be measured or ascertained in some practical way.

Categorical Variable: A variable that requires that each individual be assigned to one of several specified or implied categories, such as gender, race, or marital status.

Explanatory Variable: A variable used as a predictor in a regression equation. Sometimes referred to

Quantitative Variable: A variable that is measured numerically, such as height, blood pressure, or income.

Response Variable: The variable whose value is to be predicted.

z Score: The distance, measured in standard deviations, of a given value from the mean of a distribution.

z-Table

z	.00	.01	.02	.03	.04	.05	.06	.07	.08	.09
-3.4	.0003	.0003	.0003	.0003	.0003	.0003	.0003	.0003	.0003	.0002
-3.3	.0005	.0005	.0005	.0004	.0004	.0004	.0004	.0004	.0004	.0003
-3.2	.0007	.0007	.0006	.0006	.0006	.0006	.0006	.0005	.0005	.0005
-3.1	.0010	.0009	.0009	.0009	.0008	.0008	.0008	.0008	.0007	.0007
-3.0	.0013	.0013	.0013	.0012	.0012	.0011	.0011	.0011	.0010	.0010
-2.9	.0019	.0018	.0018	.0017	.0016	.0016	.0015	.0015	.0014	.0014
-2.8	.0026	.0025	.0024	.0023	.0023	.0022	.0021	.0021	.0020	.0019
-2.7	.0035	.0034	.0033	.0032	.0031	.0030	.0029	.0028	.0027	.0026
-2.6	.0047	.0045	.0044	.0043	.0041	.0040	.0039	.0038	.0037	.0036
-2.5	.0062	.0060	.0059	.0057	.0055	.0054	.0052	.0051	.0049	.0048
-2.4	.0082	.0080	.0078	.0075	.0073	.0071	.0069	.0068	.0066	.0064
-2.3	.0107	.0104	.0102	.0099	.0096	.0094	.0091	.0089	.0087	.0084
-2.2	.0139	.0136	.0132	.0129	.0125	.0122	.0119	.0116	.0113	.0110
-2.1	.0179	.0174	.0170	.0166	.0162	.0158	.0154	.0150	.0146	.0143
-2.0	.0228	.0222	.0217	.0212	.0207	.0202	.0197	.0192	.0188	.0183
-1.9	.0287	.0281	.0274	.0268	.0262	.0256	.0250	.0244	.0239	.0233
-1.8	.0359	.0351	.0344	.0336	.0329	.0322	.0314	.0307	.0301	.0294
-1.7	.0446	.0436	.0427	.0418	.0409	.0401	.0392	.0384	.0375	.0367
-1.6	.0548	.0537	.0526	.0516	.0505	.0495	.0485	.0475	.0465	.0455
-1.5	.0668	.0655	.0643	.0630	.0618	.0606	.0594	.0582	.0571	.0559
-1.4	.0808	.0793	.0778	.0764	.0749	.0735	.0721	.0708	.0694	.0681
-1.3	.0968	.0951	.0934	.0918	.0901	.0885	.0869	.0853	.0838	.0823
-1.2	.1151	.1131	.1112	.1093	.1075	.1056	.1038	.1020	.1003	.0985
-1.1	.1357	.1335	.1314	.1292	.1271	.1251	.1230	.1210	.1190	.1170
-1.0	.1587	.1562	.1539	.1515	.1492	.1469	.1446	.1423	.1401	.1379
-0.9	.1841	.1814	.1788	.1762	.1736	.1711	.1685	.1660	.1635	.1611
-0.8	.2119	.2090	.2061	.2033	.2005	.1977	.1949	.1922	.1894	.1867
-0.7	.2420	.2389	.2358	.2327	.2296	.2266	.2236	.2206	.2177	.2148
-0.6	.2743	.2709	.2676	.2643	.2611	.2578	.2546	.2514	.2483	.2451
-0.5	.3085	.3050	.3015	.2981	.2946	.2912	.2877	.2843	.2810	.2776
-0.4	.3446	.3409	.3372	.3336	.3300	.3264	.3228	.3192	.3156	.3121
-0.3	.3821	.3783	.3745	.3707	.3669	.3632	.3594	.3557	.3520	.3483
-0.2	.4207	.4168	.4129	.4090	.4052	.4013	.3974	.3936	.3897	.3859
-0.1	.4602	.4562	.4522	.4483	.4443	.4404	.4364	.4325	.4286	.4247
-0.0	.5000	.4960	.4920	.4880	.4840	.4801	.4761	.4721	.4681	.4641
0.0	.5000	.5040	.5080	.5120	.5160	.5199	.5239	.5279	.5319	.5359
0.1	.5398	.5438	.5478	.5517	.5557	.5596	.5636	.5675	.5714	.5753
0.2	.5793	.5832	.5871	.5910	.5948	.5987	.6026	.6064	.6103	.6141
0.3	.6179	.6217	.6255	.6293	.6331	.6368	.6406	.6443	.6480	.6517
0.4	.6554	.6591	.6628	.6664	.6700	.6736	.6772	.6808	.6844	.6879
0.5	.6915	.6950	.6985	.7019	.7054	.7088	.7123	.7157	.7190	.7224
0.6	.7257	.7291	.7324	.7357	.7389	.7422	.7454	.7486	.7517	.7549
0.7	.7580	.7611	.7642	.7673	.7704	.7734	.7764	.7794	.7823	.7852
0.8	.7881	.7910	.7939	.7967	.7995	.8023	.8051	.8078	.8106	.8133
0.9	.8159	.8186	.8212	.8238	.8264	.8289	.8315	.8340	.8365	.8389
1.0	.8413	.8438	.8461	.8485	.8508	.8531	.8554	.8577	.8599	.8621
1.1	.8643	.8665	.8686	.8708	.8729	.8749	.8770	.8790	.8810	.8830
1.2	.8849	.8869	.8888	.8907	.8925	.8944	.8962	.8980	.8997	.9015
1.3	.9032	.9049	.9066	.9082	.9099	.9115	.9131	.9147	.9162	.9177
1.4	.9192	.9207	.9222	.9236	.9251	.9265	.9279	.9292	.9306	.9319
1.5	.9332	.9345	.9357	.9370	.9382	.9394	.9406	.9418	.9429	.9441
1.6	.9452	.9463	.9474	.9484	.9495	.9505	.9515	.9525	.9535	.9545
1.7	.9554	.9564	.9573	.9582	.9591	.9599	.9608	.9616	.9625	.9633
1.8	.9641	.9649	.9656	.9664	.9671	.9678	.9686	.9693	.9699	.9706
1.9	.9713	.9719	.9726	.9732	.9738	.9744	.9750	.9756	.9761	.9767
2.0	.9772	.9778	.9783	.9788	.9793	.9798	.9803	.9808	.9812	.9817
2.1	.9821	.9826	.9830	.9834	.9838	.9842	.9846	.9850	.9854	.9857
2.2	.9861	.9864	.9868	.9871	.9875	.9878	.9881	.9884	.9887	.9890
2.3	.9893	.9896	.9898	.9901	.9904	.9906	.9909	.9911	.9913	.9916
2.4	.9918	.9920	.9922	.9925	.9927	.9929	.9931	.9932	.9934	.9936
2.5	.9938	.9940	.9941	.9943	.9945	.9946	.9948	.9949	.9951	.9952
2.6	.9953	.9955	.9956	.9957	.9959	.9960	.9961	.9962	.9963	.9964
2.7	.9965	.9966	.9967	.9968	.9969	.9970	.9971	.9972	.9973	.9974
2.8	.9974	.9975	.9976	.9977	.9977	.9978	.9979	.9979	.9980	.9981
2.9	.9981	.9982	.9982	.9983	.9984	.9984	.9985	.9985	.9986	.9986
3.0	.9987	.9987	.9987	.9988	.9988	.9989	.9989	.9989	.9990	.9990
3.1	.9990	.9991	.9991	.9991	.9992	.9992	.9992	.9992	.9993	.9993
3.2	.9993	.9993	.9994	.9994	.9994	.9994	.9994	.9995	.9995	.9995
3.3	.9995	.9995	.9995	.9996	.9996	.9996	.9996	.9996	.9996	.9997
3.4	.9997	.9997	.9997	.9997	.9997	.9997	.9997	.9997	.9997	.9998

t - Table (abbreviated)

df	.10	.05	.01
1	6.314	12.706	63.657
2	2.920	4.303	9.925
3	2.353	3.182	5.841
4	2.132	2.776	4.604
5	2.015	2.571	4.032
6	1.943	2.447	3.707
7	1.895	2.365	3.499
8	1.860	2.306	3.355
9	1.833	2.262	3.250
10	1.812	2.228	3.169
11	1.796	2.201	3.106
12	1.782	2.179	3.055
13	1.771	2.160	3.012
14	1.761	2.145	2.977
15	1.753	2.131	2.947
16	1.746	2.120	2.921
17	1.740	2.110	2.898
18	1.734	2.101	2.878
19	1.729	2.093	2.861
20	1.725	2.086	2.845
21	1.721	2.080	2.831
22	1.717	2.074	2.819
23	1.714	2.069	2.807
24	1.711	2.064	2.797
25	1.708	2.060	2.787
26	1.706	2.056	2.779
27	1.703	2.052	2.771
28	1.701	2.048	2.763
29	1.699	2.045	2.756
30	1.697	2.042	2.750
40	1.684	2.021	2.704
60	1.671	2.000	2.660
120	1.658	1.980	2.617
∞	1.645	1.960	2.576

Index